The
EDEN VALLEY
AND THE NORTH PENNINES

Eden Valley viewed from High Cup Nick. The rocks of the high Pennines are younger than those of the vale.

THE
EDEN VALLEY
AND THE NORTH PENNINES

W.R. Mitchell

Phillimore

2007

Published by
PHILLIMORE & CO. LTD
Chichester, West Sussex, England
www.phillimore.co.uk

ISBN 978-1-86077-450-8

Printed and bound in Great Britain

For
Charlie Emett

Contents

List of Illustrations

Acknowledgements

My exploration of the Eden Valley and North Pennines dates from 1951, when I began a 40-year-long editorship of *Cumbria* magazine. Boundary changes in 1974, creating the county of Cumbria, affected the pride felt by local people in what had been parts of Cumberland and Westmorland. Appleby, the old county town of Westmorland and home of many late lamented friends, relaunched itself as Appleby-in-Westmorland. *The Cumberland and Westmorland Herald*, edited from Penrith by my old friend John Hurst, kept its now outdated masthead and the loyalty of its readers.

Many of the articles I wrote in *Cumbria*, initially under the pseudonym of John Armthwaite, concerned the folk life and history of the Eden Valley. A trio of knowledgeable contacts were Bill Robson, of New Hall Farm, F.W. Parrott of Kirkby Stephen and James Whitehead of Appleby. Two other residents of Appleby who extended friendship as well as information were Gordon Wood and Dr Peter Delap. Peter, who described himself as 'doctor and deerologist', welcomed me to his home in Boroughgate. I walked and talked with Charlie Emett, a proud native of Kirkby Stephen, who told me of the so-called Jew Stone. This was raised at the source of the Eden by Squire Mounsey, who in the mid-19th century had walked the full length of the river and was keen to record the fact.

At Carlisle, half a century ago, I enjoyed the friendship of such luminaries as Ernest Blezard, who presided over the wildlife section at Tullie House. Kenneth Smith, city librarian, excited my curiosity in the ancient border struggles when he produced a plaster cast of the skull of Robert the Bruce. John Austin greatly augmented my knowledge of angling in the Eden. Eric Richardson of Nenthead provided so much information about lead mining in the North Pennines that I put it in a book. Bob Swallow advised on aspects of railway history.

Edward Jeffrey, artist, who lived in Ravenstonedale, augmented my written words with delightful drawings. Alfred Wainwright, compiler of hand-written, hand-drawn guidebooks to the fells, was a friend and inspiration. 'AW', as he was called by his friends, was known to be 'partial' to fish and chips. A photograph of him was displayed in the dining room of the Kirkby Stephen fish and chip shop, which stood at the half-way point on his celebrated Coast to Coast Walk. My knowledge of Eden Valley farming was enhanced at meetings with Jim Monkhouse of Langwathby, and Bill Robson, who farmed near Appleby.

I had friends in the media. BBC Radio Carlisle (subsequently Radio Cumbria) invited me to write a script about the evolution of the song *John Peel*, the old and new versions of which were recorded in the Civic Hall by a lusty choir known as the Men of the Fells. The first radio station, an off-shoot of Newcastle, was tucked away in an upper storey of a building across the road from the Cathedral. With Nigel Holmes I had many radio excursions into the region. On my first active association with Border Television, at Carlisle, broadcasts were in monochrome. On one programme, the camera used to film a sequence in the open air was later set up to record another item under studio conditions. To reduce the high noise level, the camera had been swaddled in clothes, including my jacket.

I extend special thanks to Carlisle City Council, Eden District Council, and those dedicated folk who staff the Tourist Information Centres at Kirkby Stephen, Appleby and Alston.

Illustrations from the following sources are cordially acknowledged: David Binns, 35, 133; Edmund Bogg, *Lakeland and Ribblesdale* (1898), 17, 19, 27, 31, 34, 46, 47, 89; S.H. Cole, 106, 122; CWAAS, in collection of Cumbria Record Office, Carlisle, 25; County Library, Carlisle, 90, 91, 144; Peter Delap, 37; Edward Jeffrey, 12, 30, 40, 50, 51, 53, 54; Lord Inglewood, 39; G.E. Pallant-Sidaway, 38; Eric Richardson collection, 77, 78, 83, 84; Carson I.A. Ritchie, 33; F.S. Sanderson, 4, 142; G. Gordon Wood, 15; Geoffrey N. Wright, courtesy of the Yorkshire Dales Society, frontispiece, 3, 14; *Yorkshire Post*, 136. Engravings by Thomas Allam from *The Northern Tourist* (1834), 49, 61, 131. Map drawn by Christine Denmead. Uncredited photographs by the author.

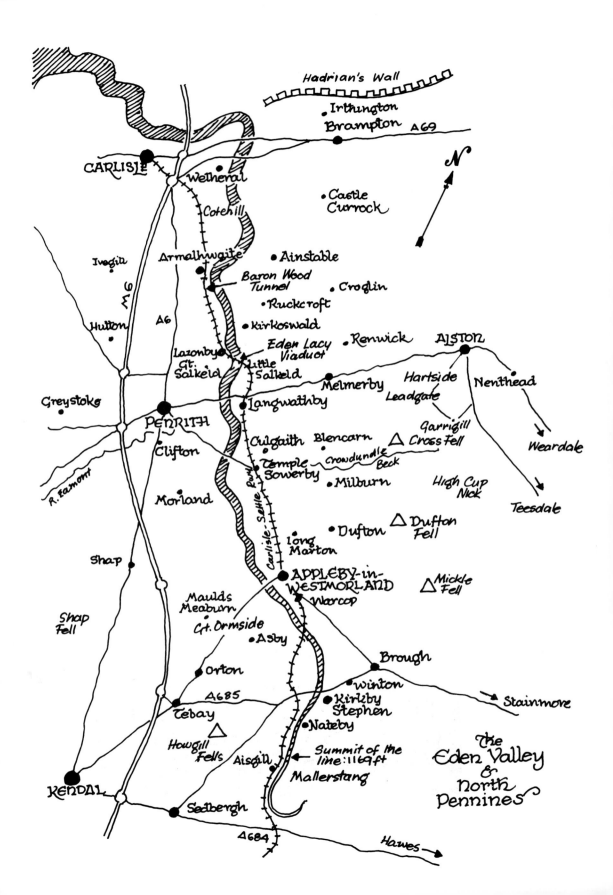

Hadrian's Wall

• Irthington
Brampton A69

CARLISLE • Wetheral

Cotehill

• Castle
Currock

Ivegill

Armathwaite • Ainstable

Baron Wood
Tunnel • Croglin

• Ruckcroft

Hutton

A6

• Kirkoswald

Lazonby Eden Lacy
Gt. Viaduct
Salkeld Little
Salkeld

• Renwick ALSTON

Greystoke

• Langwathby

Melmerby Hartside
Leadgate Nenthead

PENRITH

Clifton

Culgaith Blencarn △ Garrigill
Cross Fell Weardale

Temple Crowdundle
Sowerby Beck

• Milburn High Cup
Nick Teesdale

R. Eamont

Morland

△ Dufton
Dufton Fell

Shap

Long
Marton

APPLEBY-in-
WESTMORLAND △ Mickle
Warcop Fell

Shap
Fell

Maulds
Meaburn

Gt. Ormside

• Asby

Brough

• Orton

Winton Stainmore

A685

Kirkby
Stephen

Tebay

△ Nateby

KENDAL

Howgill
Fells

Aisgill Summit of the
line: 1169 ft
Mallerstang

Sedbergh

Carlisle–Settle Rail

The Eden Valley & North Pennines

A684 Hawes

Chapter 1

Physical Setting

The Eden Valley, opening out like a gigantic fan, merges imperceptibly with Carlisle's fertile flood-plain and, in turn, with marshland that flanks the Solway Firth. The River Eden, in its north-westward progress along the eastern rim of the county of Cumbria, has a grand setting. To the east and west are the North Pennines and the Lake District. Northwards lies the Roman Wall Country, and to the south is the Yorkshire Dales National Park. Eden, a clear river, flows through 67 miles of mainly pastoral country. Kirkby Stephen and Appleby are the main towns in the upper valley. Eden District includes the small market town of Alston situated at an elevation of 921 feet, its streets composed of stone setts and houses roofed with slabs of millstone grit. All roads lead to the border city of Carlisle, which in the boundary revisions of 1974 assumed the largest land area of any city in the country.

1 *Old Town Hall and Cross, Carlisle.*

2 *An engraving of the City of Carlisle, from* The Northern Tourist, *1834.*

The name Eden, for the river, has ancient linguistic roots and simply means 'water'. The river's source is in a spongy mass of peat and moss where Mallerstang Common drains into Black Fell Moss, two thousand feet above sea level. Eden is shorter and steeper than Swale and Ure, which have their sources in the same area but take a leisurely easterly course through Yorkshire. Hemmed in on three sides by fells, the Eden seethes through Hell Gill, a limestone gorge named after a Norse word for a cave. Michael Drayton, in his ancient and curious but entertaining poem *Poly-Olbion*, caused a wood-nymph, representing Mallerstang, to address the Eden:

> O my bright lovely Brooke, whose name doth beare the sound
> Of God's first garden-plot, th'imparadized ground,
> Wherein he placed Man, from whence by sinne he fell.

Still of modest size near Kirkby Stephen, the river gushes through a gorge named Stenkrith, on the geological boundary between limestone and sandstone. It makes a loop around Appleby and is then in relative obscurity all the way to Carlisle. Red sandstone gorges give the Eden Valley a wilderness flavour in what is otherwise an area of rich farmland. The river flows swiftly until, being joined by the River Irthing, it becomes sluggish – a river of the lowlands.

The rosy appearance of the middle and lower reaches of the valley is imparted by New Red Sandstone overlying boulder clays. The sandstone was laid down over

3 *Wild Boar Fell and the bleak fell country of upper Mallerstang. The fell was so named because the last wild boar in the locality was slain here. A boar's tooth is on display at Kirkby Stephen church.*

4 The Moorcock Inn, at a junction leading into Mallerstang.

5 *Appleby, former county town of Westmorland. In the foreground is the High Cross in Boroughgate bearing the words 'Retain your Loyalty, Preserve your Rights.'*

6 *The River Eden at Nunnery Walks is flanked by banks of red sandstone.*

a spell of 90 million years. During the arid Devonian period, which ended 350 million years ago, a dry easterly wind whipped up dunes to create a landscape similar to the modern Sahara. The desert origin of the rock is betrayed by the existence of grains of even roundness, resembling millet seed. The redness is derived from the iron content and formation under arid conditions. The sandstone, though soft and crumbly in the Appleby area, was firm and deep enough at Penrith to sustain the town's rapid 19th-century building boom.

Gypsum deposits were laid down when shallow lakes evaporated 200 million years ago. Gypsum for plaster of Paris, and anhydrite for sulphuric acid, were extracted between Little Salkeld and Glassonby until 1973. Kirkby Thore has a large gypsum-based industry, much of the material being transported here by rail, the by-product of coal-burning power stations in South Yorkshire and Staffordshire.

Eden Valley's general appearance derives more from glacial action than from erosion by the river. Outcropping limestone, a principal part of the Carboniferous series of rocks, is evident in the upper reaches. When ice sheets covered the valley to a great depth they carried ground-up rock and lumps, the 'erratics', which the melting of the ice deposited over a wide area. A major visual effect is created by 'drumlins', heaps of glacial material smoothed by ice, giving a 'basket of eggs' topography. Kirkby Stephen is drumlin country *par excellence*, with around six hundred such rounded hills.

After Temple Sowerby the Eden receives a freshwater transfusion from some notable tributaries. In the west are the Eamont, outflow of Ullswater, and the Lowther, named after an important local family. In the east, Crowdundle Beck gushes off the Pennines. Until the county boundary was re-ordered in 1974, Crowdundle Beck lay on the border between Cumberland and Westmorland. Beyond the confluence of the Eamont and the Eden, the valley is noted for its large alluvial spreads. The village of Edenhall has a name deriving from a *halk* or tract of alluvial land.

The lower reaches of the Eden frequently overspread their normal bounds, the most recent serious flooding occurring at Carlisle in January 2005. The city has suffered about fifty floods since 1800. In a massive inundation of 1571 the river created two channels around the north of the city. (In the early 19th century the old river course was filled in and the 'new' channel, known locally as 'Priests Beck' or 'Prestwick Beck', became the course of the main river.) Widespread flooding in 1771 led to a mill at Bolton near Appleby being swept away. In a spate of 1822 several bridges over the Eden, including Kirkby Stephen, were destroyed and others severely damaged.

Eden meanders over the Solway Plain, its waters blending with the Irthing from the north-east and with Petteril and Caldew from the south; they join within the boundary of the border city of Carlisle. Flooding in the area is not infrequent and the Weavers' Bank, in the Victoria and Bitts Park, west of the Eden Bridge, was formed in the 19th century through the efforts of unemployed textile workers, the object being flood protection. Under the Land Drainage Act of 1930 a River Eden Catchment Board was formed. Solway Firth is funnel-shaped and on the tidal portion of the River Eden a bore is occasionally visible. In late November 1938 nearly one thousand sheep were drowned in less than half an hour when the marshes on the Castletown estate, west of Rockcliffe, were flooded during a gale that lasted a week.

7   *Collecting gravel by Solway Firth.*

8 *Haaf net fishermen seeking salmon.*

Eden District Council, based in Penrith, takes in a vast tract of the North Pennines. To Professor C.B. Fawcett, writing in the 1930s, the North Pennine escarpment was 'probably the most impressive physical feature in England'. A.H. Griffin, a prolific writer about the northern fells, perused a map of England on which mountains over 2,000 feet were shaded and concluded that the largest mass of high land in the country was not in the Lake District, as he had supposed, but Cross Fell and its neighbours in the North Pennines: 'The Scafells, the Helvellyn range and Skiddaw are higher, but if you lumped all these fells together, toe to toe, you would still not have achieved the vast bulk of the great mountain barrier that lies to the north of Appleby.'

The name Pennines, for an uplift that became known as the spine of England, originated through a hoax. Kendall and Wroot, in their *Geology of Yorkshire*, revealed that 'Penine', first used about 1822, was adopted by the geologists W.D. Conybeare and William Philips. The name 'Alpes Penina' was derived from a Latin pamphlet, *De Statu Britanniae*, written by a monk of Westminster Abbey and purporting to describe Britain in Roman times. This document, which came to light in 1747 when Charles Bertram, a young Professor of English in Copenhagen, wrote about it to the English antiquary Stukeley, was revealed as an ingenious hotchpotch of genuine information from well-known classical sources to which great drafts of the author's imagination had been added.

Geologically, the Alston Block, some 330 million years old, occurs in repeated sequences of limestone, shale and sandstone. Its steepness is evident to those who drive up the A686 from Penrith to Alston. Climbing in a series of sharp

9 *The Moot Hall, Low Cross and St Lawrence's church, Appleby.*

zig-zags, the Hartside road levels off at almost 2,000 feet. The little town of Alston stands at the crossing point of five trans-Pennine routes, four of which ascend to around 2,000 feet before descending into the valleys of South Tyne and Nent. Alston Moor is the central feature of the North Pennine Area of Outstanding Natural Beauty, fifty square miles of fells incised by river valleys. The population of the North Pennines is around 12,000, considerably less than half that of 140 years ago when the moor was extensively mined for lead. The pattern of local settlement, including the villages of Nenthead and Garrigill, was fixed by those questing for lead.

10 Alston, a busy little town lying just north of Cross Fell, was a notable leadmining centre.

Cross Fell, at 2,930 feet the highpoint of the Pennines, has a circumference of almost thirty miles. Camden thought the name was 'an extraordinary piece of devotion, upon the planting of Christianity in these parts to erect Crosses and build Chapels in the most eminent places, as being both nearer Heaven and more conspicuous'. They were commonly dedicated to St Michael. 'That large tract of Mountain on the East side of the County [Cumberland], called Cross Fells, had the name given them upon that account for before they were called Fiend's Fell or Devil's Fell.'

In the winter of 1938 Gordon Manley (later Professor Manley, a notable meteorologist) stayed on the summit of Cross Fell for several days to study weather conditions. His base was a small hut on the walls of which ice occasionally formed to a thickness of three inches, a consequence of the deposition of rime from freezing mists. The lowest temperature recorded, 16 degrees Fahrenheit, was not as low as in the Eden Valley. There were no extremely low temperatures but instead of varying up and down, between day and night, the temperature remained constant.

On the OS map, Fiends Fell is shown as a lower feature between the summit of Cross Fell and Hartside Pass. Mickle Fell, further south, is a long grassy ridge, its sides gouged by watercourses known as 'sikes'. The western side of the North Pennines sports several pikes, or detached conical hills. Also visible from the Eden Valley is High Cup Nick, a spectacular notch in Whin Sill, a rock of volcanic origin, seen and admired by the landscape painter J.M.W. Turner when he walked by the Upper Tees, then crossed to Dufton in the Eden Valley, his route taking him along the rim. Walkers on the

11   Tan Hill Inn, *highest licensed premises in the land, between Eden and Swale.*

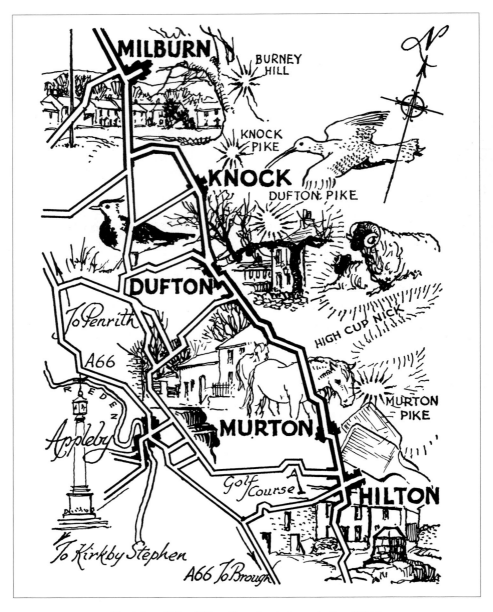

12 *Map of Eden Valley villages in relation to the East Fellside.*

Pennine Way, plodding through Birkdale to Dufton, are enlivened by the vast horseshoe precipice. R.R. Sowerby, a solicitor living at Winton, Kirkby Stephen, pondered on High Cup Nick and described it as 'a wild, eerie place'. He believed that, if dragons still existed, at least one might be found lurking hereabouts.

13   *Gordon Wood of Appleby surveys High Cup Nick, a boat-shaped gorge flanked by dolerite cliffs.*

W.T. Palmer thought the Nick bore 'a striking resemblance to the half of an empty boat'. Fan-shaped screes extend to the grey ribbon of a beck far below. Pinnacles of black dolerite will eventually be weathered to the point where they crash some eighty feet. Ravens step into an updraft and are borne aloft without beating their wings. Curiously, the Whin Sill, hard and black, lies cheek by jowl with sedimentary limestone. Francis Edge, writing about High Cup Nick in *The Dalesman* (1946), observed it as the first faint mist of an autumn twilight was blurring the steep outline. He wrote of 'a rim of rock wall in the shape of a long oval pointed at its upper end where the gill plunges through a narrow gap. Below the sheer wall of perhaps a hundred feet in depth, the sides slope very steeply for another five hundred or six hundred feet. As one moves forward along the northern rim, the steep southern slope appears almost as a vertical continuation of the upper wall, giving the impression of a sheer cliff of enormous depth.'

14   *Killhope Cross near Alston, at 2,056 feet reputedly the highest point on the English road system.*

When weather conditions are right, a wall of cloud extends along the North Pennines. An East Fellside farmer, seeing such a cloud, might remark, 'Cush, man! T'Helm Wind's on!' Manley described the Helm Wind in an article he wrote for the Eden Field Club at its twenty-first anniversary exhibition in Appleby, concluding that it may blow at any time of the year, but is most common in the springtime. 'Silverpen', a long-time journalist on the *Cumberland and Westmorland Herald*, described the Helm as the county's meteorological Public Enemy Number One, adding that the people in the affected area shared the discomforts of the communal refrigerator.

The Helm, a name that means hilltop, is created when an easterly breeze, rising and cooling on the gentle eastern slopes of the Pennines, pours down the west-facing escarpment to meet the warmer air of the Eden Valley. The Pennine escarpment thus acts like a submerged weir in a stream, a standing wave being set up just below the weir. As the Helm sweeps into the vale, there is a roaring sound, like that of the sea. Quite separate from the helm-like cloud on the fell top is the bar, pronounced 'burr' locally, a long cloud that is straight as a broomshaft. The clear sky between Helm and bar is associated with the descending air. The Helm is said never to cross the Eden. Turbulence occurs from Castle Carrock, along the East Fellside, to around Stainmore.

15 *Helm Bar, a bank of cloud resting on the edge of the North Pennines.*

Those who have lived on the East Fellside for many years distinguish between a White Helm and a Black Helm. White Helm, which occurs mainly in spring, has little moisture and tends to be prolonged. An old saying at the fellside farms asserts that if it blows for a week it will blow for three. The Black Helm, which might occur at any time, is usually accompanied by rain and, in the words of a farmer friend of mine, tends to blacken 'tatie tops, grass and leaves'. Gordon Wood of Appleby photographed two large horse mushrooms growing on the fellside above Murton; each of which had been half-peeled by the Helm Wind. Fellside sheep may suffer, either from the drying effect of the wind retarding the early growth of grass or from being entombed in drifts after snowfall.

Charles Raine, who farmed at Dufton fifty years ago, told me, 'This is one of the best farming districts in the country. The land's as good as you'll find anywhere. The Helm Wind spoils it. You can't farm against it. Almost every spring it goes with the early bite [grass]. Helm can change the whole outlook of a district overnight.' John Dargue, whose home was a wooden hut at Hilton, said that several times he had crept on his hands and knees over the edge of Meal Fell for fear of being blown backwards. A retired lead miner living at Murton told his grandson, Tommy Tinkler, there was one spell of fifteen weeks when the Helm blew every day, carrying snow with it. 'When he got home from the

16 *A round-up of sheep in the upper valley of the Tees, an area celebrated for its plant life and upland birds.*

Scorton mines, his clothes were so stiff with the cold that Grannie beat them with a stick to soften them before he could take them off.'

The folk of Nenthead, four miles from Alston, were accustomed to grim winters. If sheep began to shelter behind a plantation known as The Hush, bad weather was expected. Heavy, prolonged snowfalls occurred in 1934-5, 1941-2 and, exceptionally, in the late winter of 1947, the worst in living memory. It was a time when the snow squeaked underfoot and grouse vacated the moors, perching on walltops in the village. An old-time winter lasted from October to the end of April; a gardener would not think of planting potatoes until the middle of May. Horses had their shoes temporarily removed to be frost-sharped [sharpened] by Mr Wallace, the blacksmith, so the animals would not slither on icy surfaces. If the roads had been overblown with snow to a considerable depth, a way was cut out using a team of up to fifty men. Eric Richardson, who worked in the mines, told me he had seen snow on Cross Fell in the second week of June, and that in 1976 there were four inches of snow in his garden on the first day of June.

Chapter 2

Early History

Mesolithic (or Middle Stone-Age) man moved into Cumbria following the retreat of Pleistocene ice over 12,000 years ago. These hunter-gatherers kept to the western edge of the region. Their tools and weapons were tipped with shaped stones, or microliths. Britain was part of the continental mass until 8,000 years ago and Neolithic (or New Stone-Age) immigrants spread slowly northwards and by 4000 BC they were farming in Cumbria. The settlers cleared tracts of the wildwood with stone axes shaped from pieces of fine-grained, greenish-grey volcanic tuff, a prime source of which was an outcrop high on Pike o'Stickle in Great Langdale. Cereal crops were cultivated and animals were reared. Finds from Ehenside Tarn, including pottery, are in the museum collection at Carlisle.

About 1800 BC, groups of settlers arrived from the east, via the Tyne and Stainmore Gaps. The newcomers were a well-organised lowland people with metallurgical skills. Bronze-Age burial cairns including decorated 'collared urns' and various tools and weapons. A funeral urn discovered at Kirkoswald contained bones and a bronze pin. Few Bronze-Age artefacts have been found so assimilation with Neolithic groups must have occurred successfully. Arthur Raistrick, whose researches took in a wide area of the North West, considered that a fusion of Neolithic and Bronze-Age people gradually led to the emergence of what might be regarded as a basic 'native stock'. Hunting was combined with the rearing of cattle and sheep. Some grain was cultivated in areas of rich lowland soil.

Burial mounds and small burial circles are particularly numerous in the southern and western parts of the Eden Valley. Between 5,000 and 3,500 years ago, stone circles were erected, possibly as tribal and religious centres. Aubrey Burl, in *Ring of Stones* (1979), notes that, from the centre of the circle known as Long Meg and Her Daughters, on a spur of land above Little Salkeld, Meg herself was aligned precisely on the midwinter sunset. For many years, until 1962, a Christian service arranged by churchfolk at Addingham, and attended by the bishop, was held in the circle on the Sunday closest to Midsummer Day.

17 *Long Meg and Her Daughters, a prehistoric stone circle near Great Salkeld.*

Long Meg and Her Daughters is, strictly speaking, a stone oval with a diameter of over three hundred feet, composed of geologically differing stones. Long Meg, a sandstone monolith, is adorned by mysterious symbols: concentric circles and a curious eyebrow pattern. Burl comments: 'Such art can be seen at New Grange in Ireland. The magic symbols on Long Meg may have been made by people who had travelled across the Irish Sea during the late Neolithic period four and a half thousand years ago.' The name Meg may be a corruption of *magus* (magician) or simply a short term for a 'megalith'. Tradition associates Meg and her offspring with witchcraft. They were petrified for profaning the Sabbath with wild dancing.

Camden, the Elizabethan antiquarian, provides the first record of 'Meg with hir daughters'. The description used by Camden had been received from Reginald Bainbrigg, 'scole mister of Applebie', the first known Westmorland antiquary, of around 1600. He wrote of 'pyramides of stone, placed ther in the manner of a crown', and 'commonlie called meg with hir daughters'. Marjorie Rowling in *The Folklore of the Lake District* (1976) mentions that the original Long Meg, a noted virago of Westminster, lived in the reign of Henry VIII. 'Her name was applied to objects "of hop-pole height, wanting breadth and proportion thereto".' Rowling notes that the interest of scholars in prehistoric monuments did not begin to develop until after the Renaissance. In medieval times, interest in pagan monuments, history and literature had been frowned on by the Church.

18 *Some of Long Meg's Daughters, formed of stones with varied geological origins.*

Fanciful ideas about the big stone circle in the Eden Valley were propagated by William Langland. Celia Fiennes (1702) supported the witch theory: chip some stone from the megalith and she would bleed. William Stukeley, the antiquary, brings us back to earth with a report on missing stones in 1725, some blasted with gunpowder and others sawn up for milestones on the instructions of Colonel Lacy, a local landowner. This operation stopped abruptly when the onset of great storms terrified the superstitious workers. Marjorie Rowling wrote, 'Fear of supernatural forces doubtless prevented any resumption of the work of destruction against Long Meg and Her Daughters.'

Changes to the post-glacial climate ushered in a warm dry spell, followed after *c.*500 BC by a period when the weather was cold and wet. A considerable rise in the population of Europe led to further westward migration of Celtic folk. The so-called Iron Age (from 600-500 BC to the lst century AD) made use of a metal which represented a distinct advance on the use of bronze. A fortified site near Kirkby Stephen was grandly called Croglam Castle and a Celtic stone head was found near Appleby. A confederation of tribes in the north country, under the general title of Brigantes, had its own monarchy, gold coinage and military clout.

The Celtic period is mystically linked with a kingdom known as Rheged, its citadel said to have been in the Eden Valley, either at Carlisle or a riverside stronghold called Castle Hewen. Most of the settlements were on free-draining limestone, such as was available in the upper Eden. Groups of peasant farmers lived at farms or small settlements, their houses made of wood-and-wattle with thatched roofs. The Celtic folk were in tune with nature and named local rivers and hills. They were the people encountered by the Romans, who invaded Britain in AD 43. Emperor Claudius arrived with four legions and supporting auxiliaries, some four thousand men in all. Happily for the Romans, the Brigantes, under their queen Cartimandua, were compliant, and formed a buffer zone against the warlike Picts. The situation was destabilised in AD 71 with a rift between Cartimandua and her patriot husband Venutius. He unsuccessfully opposed the Romans, a last stand against them taking place at Stanwick.

The Romans ruled their northern territories from York, from where Pettilius Cerialis led a force that crushed a revolt by the Brigantes, according to the Roman historian Tacitus 'the most populous of all the British tribes'. The Carvetii occupied the Eden Valley, with Carlisle as a likely capital. The Roman invasion of the Eden Valley began with a march along the eastern side of the Pennines and a crossing of the cheerless moors using the Stainmore Gap. A timber fort was built at Carlisle by Petillius Cerialis in AD 72. By AD 78 Julius Agricola had led his conquering troops from Chester, via Brougham (Roman *Brocavum*) and the Eden Valley to a point as far north as the Forth-Clyde line. The north was won by the creation of a network of roads complete with forts and marching camps. The opposition was fragmented but in due course some of the former hill folk were permitted to settle on the fertile lands of the Eden Valley and the Solway Plain.

In the Tullie House Museum at Carlisle is a Roman milestone typical of the sort erected along roads at intervals of 1,000 Roman paces (1,480 metres). Found in the River Petteril, to the south of Carlisle, it is unique in that it carries the only known inscription to Marcus Aurelius Carasius, who in the year AD 287 declared Britain independent of the Roman Empire, instead of being inscribed to the reigning emperor. Six years later Marcus was murdered and any references to him were destroyed. In the case of the milestone, this was achieved by turning it over and carving a new inscription to the Emperor Constantine (AD 306-7) on the end that had previously been buried deep in the ground.

Roman *Luguvalium* (Carlisle) occupied a fine natural site on a high sandstone bluff between the Eden, on the north, and the Caldew and Petteril, west and east respectively. Good roads permitted the swift movement of men and materials. The two main links between *Luguvalium* and the eastern side of the Pennines were the Stanegate (Carlisle to Corbridge) and the Stainmore Gap, traffic on which was controlled by forts at Brough (*Verteris*) and Catterick (*Cateractonium*). Carlisle was also connected by road with a chain of coastal forts. Men drawn from all parts of the Roman world manned the four-acre fort at Brougham. A soldier was drafted from Africa to Britannia, as is evidenced by an inscribed stone at a farm on the Lowther estate, not far from Brougham. Flavius Antigonus Papias, who died at Carlisle, hailed from Greece. The Romans imposed a tax system but were inclined in some areas to take grain, livestock and hides from local farmers in lieu of money.

Thirty years after its establishment as a fort, Carlisle became an urban settlement. The Emperor Hadrian put the construction of a more permanent frontier in hand, selecting the neck of land from Wallsend to Bowness-on-Solway, a length of 73 miles (80 Roman miles). Attention shifted from *Luguvalium* to a new fort at Stanwix, on the north bank of the Eden, where a thousand-strong cavalry unit known as the *Ala Petriana* was housed. Constructed between AD 122 and 130, and well-defended, Hadrian's Wall was, according to Hadrian's contemporary biographer, constructed 'to separate the Romans from the barbarians'. Its most spectacular section is set on the crest of north-facing cliffs composed of Whin Sill.

The visual effect of the wall on ordinary people must have been awe-inspiring. Anyone approaching it from the north would see milecastles set at intervals of one Roman mile.

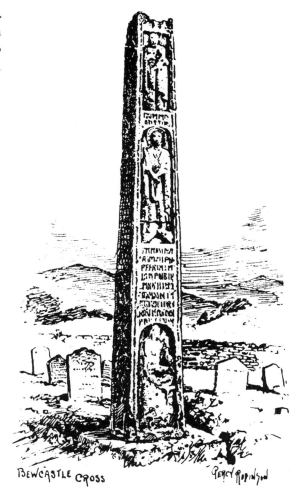

BEWCASTLE CROSS   PERCY ROBINSON

19 *Bewcastle Cross in what was North Cumberland, in a drawing by Percy Robinson, 1898.*

Between these were two turrets. Separated from the wall by a *berm*, or narrow open space, was a ditch. South of the wall what became known as the Military Way ran an unswerving course, separated from the wall by the *Vallum*, or ditch. North of the wall, forts were constructed at Netherby and Bewcastle. To the south there evolved a Romano-British society. The economy of the Eden Valley doubtless benefited from the military activity and the accompanying civilian centres, a fertile region providing much of the food.

During the fourth century AD the empire came under pressure from barbarians on its borders and the Roman army pulled back from the remoter provinces in around AD 410. Bill Rollinson, in a history of the region, wrote, 'The end

20 *Roman relics in the grounds of Tullie House, Carlisle, which had long housed the town's museum.*

of Roman rule came not with a bang but a whimper when, following a British request for aid against the barbarians, the Emperor Honorius had to tell the Britons to look after themselves.' The wall was to enchant early travellers. In 1801 William Hutton traversed it from end to end and wrote of the *Vallum*: 'I climbed over a stone wall to examine the wonder; measured the whole in every direction; surveyed it with delight, with surprise, was fascinated and unable to proceed. Lost in astonishment, I was not able to move at all.' Alfred Wainwright first saw the wall after walking along the Pennines from Settle in 1938. The sight of its 'ruinous majesty' thrilled him. Here was something that gripped the imagination till it squealed!

Following the departure of the Romans society did not collapse into chaos, and life at Carlisle seems to have continued its normal course. After pillaging by the northern tribes across the now-shattered wall had died down, a relatively quiet time ensued. Ian Richmond, a Roman scholar, having been shown two stone heads found in Northumbria, thought they represented 'with sad and awesome clarity the standards of a world which Roman had neither extinguished nor submerged'. This was the Celtic world. The old-time affinity between Cumbria and Wales endured, as evidenced when shepherds continued to use variations of a list of sheep-counting numerals: *yan, tan, tethera* and so on.

The British kingdom of Strathclyde arose in the vacuum created by the withdrawal of the legions. It covered a huge area, from Dunbarton to the Ribble – or even the Mersey. The unwieldy name *Luguvalium*, for the Border City, was corrupted in everyday use to just *leol* and prefixed by the British *ca(e)r*, or fortress, becoming Carlisle. Britons living in the enlarged kingdom of Strathclyde and Wales became known as *Cymru*, or 'fellow countrymen', from which was derived the county name of Cumberland.

The so-called Dark Ages are peopled, wrote Bill Rollinson, with 'shadowy, half-perceived figures like Arthur, Vortigern and Urien, part myth, part reality'. Urien, it is surmised, reigned over Rheged, a British kingdom established some time in the fifth century and said to have included the Eden Valley and land around the Solway Firth as far as Annan. Did Arthur represent a case of wishful thinking by a people living in fear of another wave of immigrants? There is no firm historical evidence that he ever visited Tintagel in Cornwall, where the tourist industry grew up around him, but Arthurian tales are still related there as well as in the Eden Valley and to the north of Carlisle. This most chivalrous man wields the sword Excalibur and knights in armour are seated at a Round Table. Guinevere, an alluring lady, provides feminine interest and a hint of an adulterous relationship. At Arthuret, in north Cumbria, it was believed that Arthur's last battle, at Camlann, may have begun in error when a sword was raised to kill an adder in the heather. Pendragon Castle, in Mallerstang, is associated by name with Uther, father of Arthur, whose attempt to divert the river to create a moat at the site of his castle was frustrated by two dragons controlled by Merlin. They emerged from their lair at night and ground into sand the stones set up on the previous day. Edward Gibson (1695) quoted the couplet:

> Let Uther Pendragon do what he can,
> Eden will run where Eden ran.

John Higgins, Rector of Arthuret in the early 1990s, commented that with half of Europe awaiting proof about Arthur, the absence of anything concrete was probably lending beauty to the legend. At the same time, Norma Lorre Goodrich, an American professor, bravely attempted to separate fact from Arthurian fiction. The latest of many theories about the man presumed to be a Celtic King is that he lived and died and his head was buried – Celtic style – at Arthuret, but King Arthur and his knights are of greater value to tourism as legend than as historical fact.

When in 876 the monks of Lindisfarne were driven from their island home by the Danes, they departed with a coffin containing the body of Cuthbert. For several years it was borne around the North West, including Carlisle, and at some of the stopping places churches were founded. Danes arriving from south and east, mainly from Yorkshire, firmly established themselves about Carlisle and Edenvale, naming among other places the village of Langwathby, 'village by the long ford'. What became the village greens were probably safe central corrals for cattle. Anglian settlers from Schleswig-Holstein settled in the North East and united Deira and Bernicia as Northumbria – land north of the Humber estuary. Urged to go west, some Anglian settlers filtered into the Eden Valley by the Tyne Gap and 'Stanemore', finding a landscape well suited to their type of arable and dairy farming. The names of farms and settlements ending in *-ton*, *-ham* and *-ing* signify their presence.

These were the first of the English. Their name was perpetuated in Inglewood, a major medieval landscape feature, and tucked into the flanks of the East Fellside, where becks provided a more than adequate water supply, are villages that began in this period, some of them lending their names to the associated tracts of fell-country where livestock was summered. About ten families might be housed in a typical village. The buildings were set around a green and timber palisades enclosed small crofts. Using their heavy, ox-hauled ploughs, the settlers converted woodland into fields adequate for their needs. The county name Westmorland, derived from the Anglian name *Westmaringaland*, signified the 'land of the western border'. Towards the end of the 12th century a stone called Rey or Rere Cross, by the road across Stainmore, marking the boundary between England and Scotland, might have been a Roman milestone or a memorial to Eric Blood-axe, the last Norwegian king of York who died in a battle on Stainmore in the year 954.

Arthur Raistrick wrote, 'The general pattern of farm life in the lower country remained true for a thousand years to its Anglian pattern, with the cultivated land encircling the village, which later became the manor.' In the Eden Valley it was blended with the practices of the Norse-Irish, adventurers known as Vikings after the *viks* or creeks of their Scandinavian homeland, who made their mark on the north country from AD 793 by raiding the east coast. The Anglians were agriculturalists and the Norse-Irish were pastoralists, in general taking over 'waste' areas that had not appealed to the Angles. A sheep-based economy, fairly close to the Scandinavian model, evolved in the fell-girt upper valleys. Norse folk set up single or isolated farms or an extended family might occupy a hutment at the periphery of an Anglian parish.

An analysis of place-names indicates that the Norwegians arrived in Cumbria from the west and north, from Ireland, the Isle of Man, Scotland and the Western Isles. James W. Watt, historian of Rockcliffe, where the Eden enters the Solway Firth, believed the village name sprang from the Norse *Raufr Klif*, referring to its great red cliff. In Addingham church at Glassonby, north of the Eden, are Viking and other carvings from periods up to the 12th century. Found in the river when its level was especially low in 1913, they indicate the supposed site of a village called Addingham which stood to the south of the river near what is marked as St Michael's Well on the map. The village was overwhelmed when the Eden changed its course.

In the summer months, following the tradition of transhumance, the Norse families moved with sheep and a few cattle to *shielings* or *saeters* to take advantage of a flush of grass and enable the meadow grass to grow unhindered and thus provide a store of hay for wintering livestock. A pious people, as are many who live close to the land, they would use the local church until they had the means and support to establish their own. In Kirkby Stephen church is the Loki Stone, named after a Norse god yet featuring what appears to be a bound devil. Other enduring features of this period are hogback gravestones. The hogback, shaped like a house, has a bear hugging each gable. Having been converted to Christianity, the Anglian and Norse settlers expressed their faith by building churches and, in some cases, erecting elaborately carved stone crosses, as at Carlisle and Kirkby Stephen. The finest sculpted cross is at Bewcastle, to the north of the Wall. Collingwood described it as 'perhaps the first extant masterpiece of Early English stone carving'.

The Scots migrated from Ireland around AD 500 and established themselves in Kintyre. In about 843, Kenneth MacAlpin, King of the Scots, attained the Pictish throne. Edmund of Northumbria defeated Dunmail, the last King of Cumbria, in 945 and the region was given to Malcolm, King of the Scots, remaining with him until 1032.

Chapter 3

Norman Settlement

From the departure of the Romans to the Norman Conquest, Cumbria was, in the main, part of an independent British kingdom. The Scottish domination was a brief interlude. Most of the region, which had a strong Scots-Norse element, was not accounted for when Norman scribes compiled the Domesday survey of England in 1086. There is no mention of Carlisle but a few entries from southern areas appear under Yorkshire. Gospatric, who took over Carlisle in 1070, had given it to his son, Dolfin.

The Norman presence was felt in 1092, when William II (Rufus), a man of action, travelled north with a 'great army', drove out Dolfin and added to his kingdom the 'land of Carlisle'. The Anglo-Saxon Chronicle noted, 'In this year, King William went north to Carlisle with great levies and restored the town and built the castle.' This would have been a temporary wooden affair. William established a boundary between England and Scotland and Flemings, brought over by the Normans, were settled locally, but they made little permanent difference to the make-up of the local population.

Henry I, who succeeded Rufus, visited Carlisle in 1132. Edith, his wife, was the daughter of King Malcolm of Scotland but Henry did not let the family tie prevent his being suspicious of the Scots. He strengthened Carlisle Castle and founded Carlisle Diocese, the Augustinian priory he had established at the time of his first visit being elevated to cathedral status and dedicated to the Blessed Virgin Mary. Henry II, a visitor in 1158, granted Carlisle a charter but the Scots continued to press their claim to Carlisle throughout the reigns of Richard I and King John.

Norman domination of their newly won territories was secured using castles as power bases. Originally of the motte-and-bailey style, they consisted of wooden palisades and buildings set on a large earthen mound. Between 1087 and 1091 William II, anxious to guard the Eden Valley route used by Scottish troublemakers, commissioned a string of castles at Brough, Appleby, Brougham, Penrith and Carlisle. They were rebuilt in stone at the first opportunity. Brougham Castle, by the Eamont, was on the site of the Roman fort. Among the minor

21   *Carlisle in the summer of 1794.*

22   *Carlisle Castle, as portrayed in* Lady's Magazine, *1794.*

castles was Harcla, near Kirkby Stephen. Its owner, Sir Andrew de Harcla, a supporter of Edward II, became Earl of Carlisle. (Accused of treason in 1325, he was executed.) Edward III granted a further charter to Carlisle in 1352, giving it the right to 'a free guild and a free election of their mayor and bailiffs'. Carlisle was also awarded the right to hold a Great Fair (which is still held, on 26 August, the proclamation being uttered at 8 a.m. from the steps of Carlisle Cross). A castle is not invincible, however, and in 1173 William the Lion of Scotland, failing to overrun Carlisle Castle, took those of Appleby and Brough.

Baronies, extensive feudal lordships, were bestowed on a select few Norman nobles. The Appleby area became the Barony of Appleby, but was also known as Applebyshire or Westmorland. In the reign of Henry I, the nobility was kept in check by the appointment of two sheriffs. One served in the County of Carlisle, the other was concerned with Westmorland. Under the assize system, introduced in Norman times, royal judges were sent from the King's Court to curb too independent sheriffs and to see that royal justice was available to all. (The word 'assizes' comes from the French *s'asseoir*, to sit.) Henry II, who granted Carlisle its 1158 charter, began to use these travelling or 'itinerant' judges constantly, giving them definite districts or circuits to cover. A royal command or writ sent to the sheriff and directing him to assemble the shire court preceded the royal judges.

The great lords made manors available locally for money or military support. Norman barons, in consolidating their position, bolstered trade by being prime employers of labour and purchasers of food and wine. Castle towns

23 *Appleby Castle.*

24 *Hartley Castle, Westmorland, an illustration from* Lady's Magazine, *March 1794.*

invariably became market towns, Carlisle gaining its market charter in the 13th century. Ranulph de Meschines laid out Appleby's market. The Church became conspicuous in local affairs. Morland church, the earliest surviving stone church, has Saxon as well as Norman work. Norman masonry is evident in the churches at Appleby and at Kirkby Stephen, as well as at Kirkby Thore, Milburn and Long Marton. King Oswald, who died in 642, is perpetuated in the name of the village of Kirkoswald. According to legend, he toured with St Aidan in the seventh century and at Kirkoswald stopped at a well on the site of the present church, converting the local folk to Christianity. (The well is still in use, though not for a religious purpose.)

On a much grander scale were the great monasteries. Having acquired valuable possessions and a comfortable life on earth, a Norman lord and his family were keen to guarantee a satisfying life in the next world. The fear was not so much of God but of a sojourn in Purgatory, and succour was afforded, at a cost, by the prayers of priests. So Norman lords were generous towards the Church, endowing a chantry, funding the construction of a new building or donating a tract of land to a monastic order. Naturally, a plot would be allocated as the last resting-place of the donor and his family, on whose behalf prayers would be offered in perpetuity. The monastic system had evolved in Ireland in the fifth century. From here missionaries sailed to the Cumbrian coast. In 1088 a Benedictine priory, a daughter house of St Mary's, York, was founded at Wetheral courtesy of Ranulph de Meschines, the Norman baron who had made his headquarters at Appleby. The Wetheral monks acquired a mill-bay and salmon sluices that had formerly been owned by the Lord of Crosby. Possession of them featured on a separate charter.

Three cells cut in a redstone cliff about forty feet above the water are associated by legend with Constantine III, King of Scotland. He gave up his throne in the sixth century to become a monk under St Columba and henceforth lived a hermit's life, being martyred while on a missionary journey to the Scots. The memory of this holy man is evoked by the dedication of the present church to Holy Trinity and St Constantine. In 1573, T. Monte carved the earliest known inscription on the walls of the cells. Henry VIII dissolved the priory but the gatehouse remains to indicate its former size and grandeur.

After the Augustinian priory church of St Mary at Carlisle had become the cathedral of the diocese, Aethelwold, Henry I's confessor, was appointed the first bishop of the new see in 1133. This remote region had hitherto lain within the bishopric of York and the archdeaconry of Richmond. St Mary's was gutted in a great fire that swept through the city in 1292 and a century elapsed before it was restored.

Friars, both Grey and Black, who arrived in England in the 13th century, were represented in the life of Carlisle. No grand abbeys were established in the middle or upper reaches of the Eden Valley but Shap Abbey, tucked away beside the infant River Lowther in Westmorland, was founded in about 1191 by Premonstratensian canons. Its prominent tower, which peeps from a little valley near the town, was erected in the 16th century. Lanercost, an Augustinian foundation, was destroyed in Scottish raids but rebuilt in the 13th century in Early English style. The nave is still intact and the chancel and transepts stand to their full height.

Most of the monasteries of 12th-century foundation sprang from the benevolence of Norman lords, who gifted some of their poorer land. The monks endured primitive conditions in which to pray and work but soon improved their environment and, with further grants, extended their estates, demonstrating a flair for commerce, especially with regard to their wool and mineral resources. Eventually they were serving both God and Mammon and the workers in stone, wood and metal they employed reached a high point in craftsmanship. The bishops of Carlisle had a pele tower built overlooking the River Caldew in the 13th century. Considerably altered in the 19th century, and known as Rose Castle, it has been the bishops' home for 777 years.

Chapter 4

Border Country

Carlisle was set to become the main prize in the struggle between England and Scotland. During the Anglian and Norse settlements, the Scottish kingdom of Strathclyde held much of the western end of the border. The Scots became uneasy neighbours, resisting incursions and frequently counter-attacking. Their ruler, David I, took Carlisle in 1135, extended the castle and died there in 1153. Henry recaptured the city in 1154 and ordered that a keep should be built. In 1296 the Scottish problem literally flared: Lanercost Priory was put to the torch and Carlisle subsequently came under siege.

In the following year William Wallace, having defeated an English force but failed to take Carlisle Castle, encouraged his men to plunder much of the Eden Valley. As though in response, Edward wasted the Scottish border towns the next year and captured Wallace who, convicted of treason, met a terrible end, being 'hung, drawn and quartered'. Robert the Bruce was a formidable replacement. Edward I (1239-1307), known as 'Longshanks', held his Parliament in Carlisle with Robert the Bruce in mind, and contemplated action against him.

25 *Initial letter of the Carlisle city charter of 1316, which shows the Scots unsuccessfully besieging the city.*

26   *Lanercost Priory, pillaged by the Scots.*

27   *Armorial bearings on the tomb of Lord Dacre at Lanercost Priory, a favourite resting place of Edward I, Hammer of the Scots.*

Edward, and Eleanor his queen, stayed at Lanercost for six months. Weak and frail, he was confined to his quarters for most of the time, receiving medicine from London that did him no real good. At the head of an army, he staggered to the marsh at Burgh near Carlisle on which Lanercost had some ancient rights, but the Hammer of the Scots died in the arms of his servants within sight of the blue hills of Scotland; he was 68 years old. A monument to him has been a feature of Burgh Marsh for three hundred years. When the present pillar was raised in 1803, on the instructions of the Earl of Lonsdale, an inscription in Latin was included but a local man plaintively asked, 'Who's gang to read it?' Railings round the monument were placed there to prevent cattle rubbing against it.

On becoming the Scottish king, Robert the Bruce led an army that trounced the English at Bannockburn in 1314, making it impossible for the English to police the Borders. The Bruce made two attempts to take Carlisle but encountered an impregnable defence. In a foul mood, he led his men on a plundering expedition that extended to Furness Abbey near the shore of Morecambe Bay. The prime access point to England by a western route was through the yawning mouth of the Eden Valley and in 1314 the settlements of Brough and Appleby were destroyed. In 1315, when the Bruce had put Carlisle under siege, Sir Andrew de Harcla and his 'Kendal archers, all in green' defended the city. Robert disengaged 11 days later, his army leaving their equipment behind. But memories of valiant deeds were short, and in 1338 Sir Andrew was unjustly hanged at Harraby.

From the 14th to the 17th centuries, the western part of the border between England and Scotland was turbulent and lawless. An indistinct borderline to the north of Carlisle gave rise to the term Debatable Lands, and raids by the Scots had a debilitating effect on Eden Valley life. Mannix and Whellan (1847) wrote in their potted history of Cumberland, 'The Borders ... were ... accustomed to the most nefarious practices of freebooting and considered theft and plunder only as a fair reprisal.' The freebooters 'entertained but little affection for the nations to which they respectively belonged for it was a matter of the utmost indifference to them whether they preyed upon the opposing frontier or upon their own countrymen.'

28 *Kenneth Smith, Carlisle librarian, with cast of the skull of Robert the Bruce.*

29   *Pendragon Castle.*

30   *Pendragon Castle, painted by Edward Jeffrey. The Scots destroyed Pendragon in 1341.*

At Clifton by the Lowther, said to have been one of the resting places of the body of St Cuthbert at the time of Danish raids on Lindisfarne, land values plummeted. The church, worth £10 in Papal Taxation for 1291, had its value reduced by the ravages of the Scot and in 1318 was worth a mere £1. At Edenhall the value of the benefice was reduced between 1291 and 1318 from £24 1s. 4d. to £6 13s. 4d. per annum. In about 1450, a tower with dwarf spire and battlements was added at the west end of the church. When in 1338 Edward III demanded the settlement of taxes by Westmorland wool, he was informed that 'the clergy are well nigh ruined by the fury of the Scots, and [the bishop's] own few sheep have almost totally perished in enemy raids'.

In the Eden Valley, the rich man had his castle. A cheaper alternative for lesser lords was a modification of the Norman keep designed to withstand short sieges. This was a pele, from 'palisade', the earliest form of local defence. Pele towers were being constructed from the mid-14th century and the style persisted until the beginning of the 17th century. Fifty-eight such towers were noted by Sir Nikolaus Pevsner in the Cumberland and Westmorland volume of *The Buildings of England* series. A typical pele was square and three-storeyed with walls between 3½ and 6 feet thick. It had limited access at ground level and small windows. The vaulted ground floor might, in an emergency, accommodate livestock. The first floor offered living accommodation for servants and also a kitchen. The master and his family lived and slept on the top floor. Access was available to a lead roof, so a broad view of the surrounding countryside was possible. The strong western tower of St Cuthbert's church at Great Salkeld, dating from c.1380, served to house the bells and, if there were the prospect of a Scottish raid, as a pele providing sanctuary to the people. The church tower at Burgh-by-Sands has pele-like features: stout walls built partly of recycled Roman stone,

31 *Drawing of pele tower at Clifton. This form of defence was vital during Scottish raids.*

and a narrow door secured by a stout bar. There was safety in a pele until the raiders had collected sufficient loot or, becoming bored, had moved on.

During the Scottish threat, many fine old properties in the Eden Valley had a pele at their core or attached to the house. At Hutton-in-the-Forest a tower of 14th-century date, complete with moat and drawbridge, was constructed about a century after a visit by Edward I, but within two years of Union the de Huttons had sold their property to Sir Richard Fletcher of Cockermouth, who filled in the moat, disposed of the drawbridge and 'made ye house and seat more pleasant'. A 15th-century pele tower is the oldest part of The College at Kirkoswald, the name referring to priests who were housed here from 1523 until the Dissolution. The College subsequently became, and still is, the home of the Fetherstonhaugh family. At Yanwath, named after a ford over the Eamont, and at Wharton Hall, near Kirkby Stephen, additional buildings were arranged around a *barmkin*, or courtyard.

Yanwath's substantial tower was constructed in 1322 on the orders of John de Sutton, and owned by the Threlkeld family from the time of Edward I to Henry VIII. A *barmkin* was added when the property passed by marriage to Lord Dudley in 1512. The Dudleys owned Yanwath until 1654, then sold it to the Lowthers, who have owned it, virtually unchanged, to this day. Standing 55 feet high, the tower has a vaulted basement and walls that are six feet thick. Machell, writing in the 17th century following a visit to Yanwath, noted that it 'hath a delicate prospect when you are at it, and hath the grace of a little castle when you depart from it'. At Clifton is a good example of an unaltered (but well-restored) pele; it was built in later times to a height of 37 feet, with walls three feet thick.

In 1463 Edward IV made a truce with Scotland and his brother, the Duke of Gloucester, became Warden of the West Marches. While England and Scotland were theoretically at peace, border life was turbulent. The area was undeveloped, a half-empty landscape where even a modest settlement might bear the name of town. By this time minor cattle raids were being made both ways. The year 1552 saw the delineation of the western end of the border. George MacDonald Fraser, in *The Steel Bonnets* (1971), graphically described life in the old Border Marches. The turbulence reached its peak in the 16th century, when 'great numbers of the people inhabiting the frontier territory lived by despoiling each other'. The great border tribes, both English and Scottish, 'feuded continuously among themselves'. The social system involved raiding, arson, kidnapping, murder and extortion. In general, the Border Marches were beholden neither to English nor Scottish law and what law existed was invoked to deal with endemic crimes of raiding and rustling. Fraser's book tells the story of the steel-bonneted Anglo-Scottish Border Reivers. Derived from every social class, they had a professional attitude towards cattle- and horse-rustling, usually arriving at night. Their activities were

32 *Yanwath, with additional house. This pele tower, on the Lowther Estate, has preserved most of its original features.*

romanticised in border ballads. When times were good, reiving was regarded as a sport; in grim times, it was a struggle for existence. In the Debatable Land, the Armstrongs, Forsters and Routledges were on the rampage so often that such behaviour was accepted as part of life – or death.

When, in 1568, the wistful, ill-fated Mary, Queen of Scots, out of favour and defeated in Scotland, sought sanctuary in Carlisle Castle, she was given freedom to worship in the cathedral, and to hunt. After two months' imprisonment, she was led to further captivity at Bolton Castle in Wensleydale. During a truce in 1596, the English captured Kinmont Willie, a Scotsman with a lively disposition. He was imprisoned at Carlisle Castle, but not for long. On the stormy night of 13 April, a Scottish rescue party crossed the swollen River Eden and released him. His pursuers were said to have jibbed on reaching the riverbank. The memories of Kinmont Willie's escape have not been allowed to fade and live on in song and story.

The end of the reivers occurred during the reign of King James I of England, who appointed Lord Hume as lieutenant of the three Scottish Marches and made George Clifford, Earl of Cumberland, responsible for the English side. They took over in the autumn of 1603 and before long the hangman was busy despatching members of the most notorious local families, including Elliotts and Armstrongs. Members of the Graham family were transported to Ireland but contrived to return surreptitiously. A Victorian addition to their home at Netherby was a life-sized statue of a Moss Trooper, complete with sword and spur found on Solway Moss, where a skirmish between English and Scots had taken place in the 16th century.

James W. Watt, consulting the parish register at Rockcliffe at the mouth of the Eden, discovered that some names persist while others disappear. 'After the Border lost its significance, we find Scottish surnames mixing up with the Cartners, Wilkins, Nixons and Jacksons. A few of the names have a strange sound to me – Sultis (can this be Salthouse?), Ardis, Mallabar and Hilan. A Scottish cooper named James Greer, mentioned by the historian Hutchinson, is entered in the register as having been buried on 12 May 1795, at the age of 107 years.'

The stormy days were not yet over for Carlisle. Besieged during the Civil War in 1644-5, its Royalist citizens endured their miserable and hungry state, subsisting for a while on rats, dogs and linseed meal. Only when they heard of the Royalist defeat at Naseby did they capitulate to the Parliamentarians who, being Presbyterian Scots and keen to hold what they had gained, repaired the castle, taking stone from the abbey buildings and from the residences of the canons. When they were still short, they promptly pulled down six bays of the cathedral nave. Sir Philip Musgrave took the castle for the King three years later, surrendering it in the same year to a Parliamentarian force flush with their success at Preston. Carlisle, the base for forays into Scotland, had a garrison consisting of 800 infantry and 1,200 cavalry.

In 1745, the citizens of Carlisle heard the skirling of the bagpipes as Prince Charles Edward Stuart entered Carlisle with a Jacobite army. At Carlisle Cross, the Prince proclaimed his father King of England. The Cumberland Militia, called out to defend the city, ignominiously capitulated. In December 1745 troopers of the Duke of Cumberland's Bland's regiment and those of Bonnie Prince Charlie met on Clifton Moor, and a skirmish followed. A simple headstone in the graveyard adjacent to Clifton church commemorates those who fell. The burial register notes, 'The 19th Dec. 1745 10 Dragoons to wit six of Blands three of Cobhams and one of Mark Kerrs Regiment buried who was killed ye evening before by ye rebels in ye skirmish between ye Duke of Cumberland's army and them at ye end of Clifton Moor next ye town.' The seven Highlanders who perished were buried at Town End. It is believed that in about 1860, when the railway was being constructed, the remains of the hapless Scotsmen were disturbed and moved to the churchyard.

Leaving a small garrison, the Prince advanced from Carlisle as far as Derby. When next the citizens of Carlisle saw his retreating supporters they were a shattered remnant of the force that had gone south. The Jacobites were to be routed at Culloden, where their nemesis became known as Butcher Cumberland. Several members of the Cumberland Militia who had enrolled in Cumberland's army were in the victorious force at Culloden, and prisoners from the battle were quartered in Carlisle Castle and Cathedral. Others were hanged at Harraby or transported.

33 *The Duke of Cumberland was portrayed in triumph on a special coin featuring Carlisle. On the reverse are the words 'You bring back peace to troubled minds.'*

The border became quiet in the 17th century following improvements in cattle management, such as over-winter feeding, and it was left to writers like Sir Walter Scott to romanticise the gory past. Smuggling across the Solway was featured in his novel *Guy Mannering*. Robbie Burns, Scotland's national poet, was for a short time a Revenue officer, one of several strung out along the Solway coast. Before the Act of Union was passed, the Revenue men had focused their attention on those who smuggled goods from Scotland. Subsequently, in secluded Solway, the concern was with smugglers based in the independent Isle of Man, who used sloops and cutters. Those officers who were landlubbers had to become familiar with the quicksands and marshes. Robbie Burns was in the forefront of a party of Revenue men and dragoons who made for a becalmed lugger and was the first to board the vessel. This was sailed to Dumfries, condemned as a seizure and sold.

Smuggling flourished in the early part of the 19th century. Until 1825 England placed a heavy duty on salt and the Scottish duty on whisky was, until 1855, a fraction of that in England. Whisky was ferried over the Esk, thence across the Eden in bladders attached to specially trained dogs. Smuggling ended when the national duties were equalised.

Chapter 5

Inglewood Forest

In 1092 William II, having taken over Carlisle and north-west England and now keen to make the northern marches more secure, planted colonists from Normandy and Flanders on the lands of Inglewood, 'the forest of the Angles', which he had classified as a royal forest. The intrusion was limited to a few places near Carlisle. *Engla wudu*, as the name appeared in the register of Holme Cultram Abbey after 1150, appealed to a Norman lord because of the hunting possibilities. This was the resort of fallow deer, wild swine, 'all manner of wild beasts', and hawks that might be trained for falconry.

Inglewood was a vast triangular area between Carlisle and Eamont Bridge bounded by (though not including) Caldbeck in the west and the River Eden

34 *Lanercost Priory was used by Edward I and his barons as a base from which to hunt wild boar and red deer in Inglewood.*

in the east. Under the Normans, it was counted among the great forests of England. It became the largest when, in the reign of Henry II, the forest was extended eastwards to the foot of the Pennines. In landscape terms, Inglewood was a plateau of carboniferous limestone dominated in the east by a string of sandstone hills. The limestone did not obtrude, having been plastered with boulder clay by a glacier that trundled northwards, sculpting the Eden Valley. So thick was the clay that when the drainage system was established the principal rivers, Caldew and Petteril, debouching into the Eden near Carlisle, did not erode it to bedrock. The highspots of eastern Inglewood were Barrock Fell, Blaze Fell and Lazonby Fell, plus a prominent slab of high ground that would become known as Penrith Beacon.

Inglewood was not an undisturbed wilderness when first viewed by the Normans. The area had been inhabited by Anglian settlers from Northumbria, who arrived during the seventh and eighth centuries, farming strips of open fields. Once it had been declared a royal hunting ground, Inglewood was administered under the forest law that a king might make or change at will. Through possession of Inglewood, he also controlled a large part of a region in which barons might operate independently. The existence of the forest system was not to their liking.

In the 12th century, one Walter Mapin bemoaned the fact that William had taken away so much land from God and man, sacrificing it to wild beasts and hunting dogs. In the closing years of the 11th century, William had organised the creation of Plumpton Hay, a deer park of some 2,500 acres, by fencing off land between the River Petteril and the eastern bounds of Skelton. Chroniclers were fond of exaggerating and rounding up the figures for game slain by the mighty. When Edward I hunted over four days, the toll on the first day alone was reportedly four hundred harts and hinds.

Inglewood was renowned for the quality of its oak trees and the king permitted some of them to be despatched to the Bishop of Ely during the construction of the cathedral tower. Regarders, who were 12 knights charged with making a survey every three years, monitored changes in the forest such as tree clearing, planting and even the number of bee swarms. Members of the de Raughton family were

35 *Peregrine falcon, a species venerated by Norman lords who, fond of falconry, protected the birds in Inglewood.*

classified as regarders, holding land by service of 'keeping the eyries of hawks in the forest of Inglewood'.

The hand of authority fell heavily on those who violated the forest laws. It was an offence for unauthorised persons to carry bow and arrows in the forest. The presence of a dog was legal only if a warrant had been issued. In the reign of Henry III, a greyhound owned by a Carlisle man was used to take three deer, three men unleashing the animal between Kirkoswald and Greystoke. Adam Turpe of Edenhall, a noted deer-stealer, was one of those who commonly chased the deer beyond the Eden by moonlight. Adam de Langrigg killed a hind as food for his wedding feast.

The Warden, chief administrator of Inglewood, had an hereditary position and was selected from the family with the diminutive barony of Burgh-by-Sands, lying between the forest and the sea. He was not powerful enough to upset the political stability, but there were perks. In Inglewood he might hunt game, except deer and boar (which were reserved for the king), and he held the rights to the fishing, to honey and to the bark and stumps of timber. To help protect deer in the fawning season, he might claim any swine that escaped during the 14 days before and after the feast of St John the Baptist.

Three types of court existed. The woodmote was held every 40 days. A Middle English romance bearing the name *Arthur* connects Carlisle with Inglewood, mentioning 'three yeomen of the North Country':

> The one of them was named Adam Bell,
> The other Clym of the Clough,
> The third was William of Cloudesley,
> An archer good enough.
> And if you go to Carleile brother,
> And from this wild wood wend,
> If that the Justices may you take,
> Your life were at an end.

A poacher committed by the verderer at the woodmote might be fined at the justice-seat in Carlisle. Only the King and the Justice of the Forest were permitted to release a prisoner on bail for slaying deer. Outlawry was the consequence of a much more serious matter, such as failing to turn up at court. The most distinguished poachers were lords of manors and the clergy. In 1256 the Bishop of Carlisle, with greyhounds, 'took' a hart and a hind at Plumpton. The venison was carried back to Rose Castle, the episcopal palace.

The swainmote, which met on the Feast of St Barnabas (11 June) before a venerable thorn tree at the northern end of the parish of Hesket, came under the jurisdiction of the verderers and four gentlemen of good fame and learning in

36   *Inglewood was not a forest in the modern sense but a chase in which wild creatures were hunted. This stag, a blend of fell-going and park stags, was photographed at Lowther.*

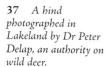

37   *A hind photographed in Lakeland by Dr Peter Delap, an authority on wild deer.*

the forest law. The forest was divided into three wards, each having a hereditary forester-in-fee who appointed and paid the foresters and gamekeepers. In the morning the swainmote dealt with affairs relating to the Nether (north) and West Wards. Matters relating to the Over Ward (south) came under consideration in the afternoon. Disputes were tried and tenants attended to pay their annual dues to the lord of the forest.

Thomas de Multon, forester-in-fee during the reign of Henry III, appeared at an inquisition into his claim to ancestral privileges as hereditary forester. Held in Carlisle, it provides an insight into his special position. He was entitled

38 *Interior of cruck house at Cross Farm, Burgh-by-Sands, a form of dwelling used for many years and reconstructed in a drawing by G.E. Pallant-Sidaway.*

to payment for all escaped animals except swine, for which there were special payments. He had a right to take all dead wood, standing or fallen, dry wood and all timber not producing food. De Multon claimed 'all honey with its wax throughout the whole of the King's demesne wood', as well as pannage of swine. The right of fishing 'throughout the whole of the King's forest in all waters and woods' was also his.

These courts tried offences but did not have the authority to judge or punish the miscreants. It was at the third type of court, known as the justice-seat and held in Carlisle, that punishment was meted out by the Chief-Justice in Eyre, a judge of the forest law. There were two such judges in England, one for the forests north of the Trent and the other for those to the south.

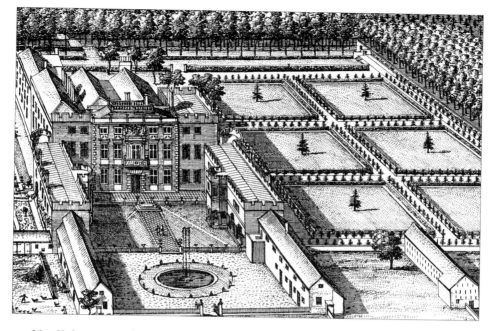

39 *Kip's engraving of Hutton-in-the-Forest, c.1700. The principal house began life as a pele tower.*

More insidious than poaching was the effect on Inglewood of those who surreptitiously absorbed fringe areas for farming. Stringent rules related to pannage (grazing rights) and assarting (the conversion of woodland to cultivated land), yet farmers nibbled all the time at the boundaries of the forest, taking in new land.

Inglewood oaks formed the framework for many of the old clay 'dabbins', the cottage dwellings most typical of the clayey Cumberland Plain. Straw was available from the strips of cultivation and thatching material was at hand in the reeds and rushes of un-reclaimed swamps. Ernest Blezard, long at Tullie House Museum, Carlisle, described the 'dabbin' to me. It was cruck-built in a style that may have been around before the end of the 14th century or whenever it was that strong timbered cottages began to replace the flimsy cabins and hovels of medieval times. The crucks, which were the main timbers, were set up in pairs to support the roof-tree at their meeting point. An evenly matched pair was occasionally got from a suitable trunk split full length. Blezard remembered a violent storm that battered a clay building at Burgh-by-Sands and exposed the tips of the crucks. They did not meet but were spaced a little apart by tie pieces on which the ridgepole rested. He was told that this kind of construction showed a Scandinavian influence. The clay 'dabbin' was finished inside and out with a coating of limewash. 'That essential part of it, the inglenook, holding a settle on either side of the hearth, was one of the cosiest corners ever devised against the cold of winter nights.'

The forest system in its original form lasted for about two centuries. Clearances were authorised by the Crown. During the Wars of the Roses, the controlling supervision of the system became lax. Legal and hunting controls were at an end by the close of the 16th century. The courts of the royal forests were abolished in 1817, and two years later 28,000 acres of the forest were enclosed. The present neat landscape of rectangular fields and roads unfolding in long, straight lines emerged.

James Losh, a lawyer from Newcastle who had been brought up at Wreay, visited Inglewood in the 1820s when it was being overlaid by a grid of roads. After riding from Brougham to Carlisle, he noted that 'the country is greatly improved not only by the enclosure of Inglewood Forest but also by the formation of the new roads, growth of trees and improved cultivation of the country in general. The change is so great that I actually lost my way in a district with which I was familiar as a boy.' Formerly wooded areas are recalled by place-names: Lutham (Ludham, the grove farm), Udford (wood-ford, over Eamont) and Oxhouse Oaks.

Among the oak trees venerated through age and association was the Hartshorn Tree, which stood by the old Roman road near Brougham being described to me by Mrs Barbara Pollock of the Winderwath estate. She intended to plant an oak where the famous old tree had stood. It was named Hartshorn because of the antlers attached to it, said to be those of a hart-of-grease (a stag aged eight) which had been pursued by a deerhound known as Hercules in 1333. A chase that began at the tree extended to Red-Kirk in Scotland and back, rather more than eighty miles in a single day. The traditional tale relates that back at the tree the hart leapt over the fence of the park and promptly died. The hound dropped dead just before reaching the fence. The horns remained in situ until 1658, local people chanting that,

> Hercules killed Hart-o-Grease,
> And Hart-o-Grease killed Hercules.

Mannix and Whellan (1847) noted that a 'time-honoured' oak standing on Wrangham Moss and known as 'the last tree of Inglewood Forest' had 'weathered the blasts of upwards of 800 stormy winters'. For over 600 years it had marked the boundary between the manors of the Duke of Devonshire and the Dean and Chapter of Carlisle. A local hermit called John de Corbig 'counted his beads beneath its shade'. The oak fell from sheer old age on 13 June 1823.

Chapter 6

Great Families

For over three centuries, the Cliffords dominated the Craven district of Yorkshire and the county of Westmorland. Robert, who served on the Welsh then the Scottish Marches, was the first illustrious person to bear the name Clifford. He had the Honour of Skipton granted to him in 1311 but three years later was slain at Bannockburn. A Clifford had been present at the death of Edward I on Burgh Marsh and the family had representatives at other notable battles, including Crecy and Agincourt. Support was given to the Lancastrian cause in the Wars of the Roses and a Clifford took a contingent of Craven men to Flodden Field. Their special reward, in the reign of Henry VIII, was the earldom of Cumberland.

The most prominent of the Cliffords in the Eden Valley context was a woman, Lady Anne, the last of her line. Acknowledging that 'time brings to forgetfulness', she recorded everything of consequence in her diary or had it chiselled on stones wherever her generosity led to a restoration project. She raised an ornate pillar at the roadside near Brougham to mark the spot where she bade a last farewell to her mother. Martin Holmes of Appleby, an authority on the Elizabethan period, referred in *Proud Northern Lady* to the popular image of Anne as an autocratic and terrifying old person with a caustic tongue, and concluded it was not merited. A brusque and discourteous letter attributed to her by Horace Walpole in 1753 was discredited as an 18th-century fabrication.

Lady Anne, twice (unhappily) married, twice widowed, was proud of her family and

40 *Drawing of Lady Anne Clifford.*

proud of her status as Countess Dowager of Dorset, Pembroke and Montgomery, Baroness Clifford, Westmorland and Vesey, Lady of the Honour of Skipton-in-Craven and Hereditary Sheriffess of Westmorland. As the sole but female heir, entitled to inherit the family estates on the death of her father, George, 3rd Earl of Cumberland, she was shocked to discover he had illegally willed the barony of Clifford to his brother, Sir Francis, from whom it descended to his sole male heir. On their deaths, and after a legal battle spanning 41 years, Anne came into her inheritance in Craven and Westmorland. With the Civil War raging, she wisely remained in London until it was safe to visit her northern inheritance. Then, in the summer of 1649, aged 59, she travelled north on a tour of inspection and in the same year put in hand repairs to Skipton Castle, a Royalist stronghold that had been subjected to Parliamentary siege. She had been at the court of Elizabeth and James I, and in later years dressed herself in black serge, 'more coarsely and cheaply than most of the Servants in her House'. Her petticoat, made locally, cost her less than 40 shillings. Most of her leisure time was passed in reading, listening to music and embroidery.

Anne went on a post-Civil War building spree that began in 1649 and was completed 15 years later. Sir Nikolaus Pevsner, architectural historian, alluded to her 'romantic passion for castles', which did not appeal to Cromwell who saw in them the possibility of a threat. She ignored him, and one suspects he grew to admire the indomitable little lady. She also restored churches and on a rafter of the Lady Chapel in the south aisle of Appleby church was carved 'Ann Covntess of

41   *The Countess Pillar near Brougham was raised by Lady Anne Clifford at the point where she bade her much-loved mother a last farewell.*

Pembroke in Ano 1655 repaired all this bvilding.'

The almshouses in Boroughgate were provided in memory of her mother, and endowed with land 'for the yearly maintenance of a Mother, a Reader and Twelve Sisters for ever'. Each sister was provided with a house, and the facilities updated with the passing of time. The Charter of Incorporation states, 'In the Northern parts and particularly near our Borough of Appleby there are very many women decrepit and broken down by old age who are supported by begging their bread and being without any receptacle or relief lead an idle or vagrant life.' Included in the scheme was a chapel, to which Anne presented a chest where the title deeds of properties from which revenue was drawn might be lodged. She

42 *One of the faces of the Countess Pillar near Brougham.*

adorned the place with carved shields of arms relating to her connection with the Vipont and Clifford families, while displayed on each side of the entrance were the arms of her two husbands impaling her own.

Lady Anne gloried in travelling on routes where coaches had been previously unknown. The Old Highway from Cotterdale to Mallerstang was a case in point and the party encountered 'a great storme of Raine and wind'. Anne undertook a hundred-mile journey from Skipton-in-Craven to her Eden Valley castles, travelling in medieval splendour in a coach drawn by six horses and accompanied on board by 'my two gentlewomen and my woman servants'. Menservants travelled on horseback. Her domestic entourage was in attendance. On the leg of a journey ending at Pendragon Castle in Mallerstang, Lady Anne was 'accompanyd on the way by severall of the gentry of the County and of my Neighbours and Tennants, both of Appleby, Kirkby Stephen and Mallerstang.'

She was generous to the needy and made gifts to friends, some receiving a copy of a favourite portrait. Huge door locks made by George Dent, a craftsman of Appleby, at £1 each were fitted to Asby Rectory, Dacre church, Dalemain and Rose Castle, the residence of the bishops of Carlisle. Anne died in 1676 aged 86. After a grand funeral in Appleby church, her coffin of lead fitted with iron handles was carried down a flight of eight steps into a vault of modest size, 9ft 2in square, strongly arched with stone to the height of 6ft 2in. Fluted lengthwise, the coffin bore, in addition to a commemorative brass plate, the figure of a face and body terminating at the chest.

The Earls of Thanet inherited Pendragon Castle, on which Anne had bestowed so much love and money. Her favourite grandson, Thomas, 4th Earl of Thanet, not wishing to pay for the upkeep of several castles, dismantled Pendragon in 1685. Salvaged materials – stone, timber, lead from the roof – were sold or taken to Skipton Castle. Brough Castle was also used as a quarry.

Like the Cliffords, the Musgrave family arrived in England with the Conqueror. They became one of the great border families, Sir Thomas Musgrave, the first member of the family to own Hartley, dying in 1376. Following the change of ownership, the Hartley Chapel at Kirkby Stephen church became known as the Musgrave Chapel. Sir Richard de Musgrave, who died in 1409, is reputed to have slain the last wild boar in the locality. Sir Richard and his lady shared the same tomb, and when it was opened in 1847 the tusk of a wild boar was found on his breast.

The Musgraves took their name from two villages, one on each side of the River Eden. A warlike lot, they lived at Musgrave and Harcla Castles respectively. Having acquired the Edenhall estate near Langwathby by marriage into the Stapleton family in 1468, they resided there in grand style for over four centuries, prominent in local life as baronets and sheriffs, soldiers and Members of Parliament. Musgraves fought on the Royalist side during the Civil War. The Luck of Edenhall, a treasured possession, was a cup of yellowish glass with red, blue, green and white enamel and gilt. Made about 1250 at Aleppo in Syria, it may at one time have been used as a chalice. It was believed that were the Luck to break or fall, good fortune would desert the family. Sir George Musgrave, who presided over Edenhall in mid-Victorian days, was aware of the necessity of taking care of the Luck but, as T.A. Trollope discovered, was keen to show it off whenever he had visitors. He allowed them to handle and examine it, maintaining 'that otherwise there was no fair submission to the test of luck, which was intended by the inscription'. (The vase has long had safe accommodation in the Victoria and Albert Museum in London.)

A new Edenhall was built in 1821 to a design by Sir Robert Smirke, the architect of the British Museum. Its amenities included, as a novelty, piped water. Wages for the estate workers were low but villagers paid no rent or rates. The hall was subsequently occupied by the Shaw family for thirty years, then became a school, but was demolished and sold piecemeal in 1934. Miss Harriet Airey, whom I met in 1954, began work at Edenhall aged thirteen. The daughter of one of the villagers who had worked in the kitchens of Edenhall for a shilling a day, Harriet became fourth housemaid and was employed by Sir Richard Musgrave,

43 *Musgrave Monument at Penrith.*

the last of his family to occupy the premises. Miss Airey's father, David, was 'gasman', his task being to attend to the gas plant installed in a small detached building in July 1876. There remain at Edenhall the courtyard and surrounding red sandstone buildings, of which a clock tower is the dominant feature.

The Whartons were prominent in the life of the upper Eden Valley for five centuries. In about the 14th century they moved from Lammerside Castle to Wharton Hall, which is set back from the high road to Sedbergh from Kirkby Stephen. Richard Wharton's design for the hall followed the normal plan, a central hall with private apartments at one end and domestic offices at the other. Being within easy raiding distance of the border, the apartments were set in a strong tower. Rather more than a century later, Thomas Lord Wharton (1495-1568) added a banqueting hall and a new west wing that contained the fashionable Elizabethan Long Gallery. Such improvements befitted Thomas's status as Lord Warden of the Marches. He was serving as Captain of Carlisle Castle in 1542 when, aided by a force commanded by Sir William Musgrave, he surprised and routed a greater Scottish force ensconced on Solway Moss. Around 1,500 prisoners were taken.

Three years later, with Lord Dacre, Wharton sacked Dumfries, an achievement that led to his being created the 1st Baron Wharton in 1544. He founded the

44   *Drawing of Wharton Hall, 1773.*

45   *Philip, Duke of Wharton, as illustrated in* Pennant's Tour.

grammar school at Kirkby Stephen in 1566, endowing it with a rectory house and an annual rent of £20. Wharton decreed that 'the schoolmaster, every working day at the least, shall begin to teach from six o'clock in the morning in summer and from seven o'clock in the winter; and so shall continue teaching until eleven o'clock. The self same thing shall he diligently do after dinner from one o'clock till six in summer and five in winter.'

When Sir Thomas Warton died, in 1568, he was buried alongside his two wives, Eleanor Stapleton and Ann Talbot. The tomb, in the Wharton Chapel at Kirkby Stephen, is adorned by a full-length figure clad in armour and flanked by his two wives, described by local historian Sowerby as 'stern, hard-faced women'. (The tomb is empty, the trio being interred in a similar tomb at Healaugh, near Tadcaster.) Chancellor Burn, Vicar of Orton, believed that the bull's head carved under Wharton's head on the family crest amusingly paraphrased the Latin inscription:

> Here I Thomas Wharton do lie
> With Lucifer under my head;
> And Nellie my wife hard by,
> And Nancy as cold as lead:
> Oh, how can I speak without dread!
> Who could my sad fortune abide?
> With one devil under my head
> And another laid close on each side!

Thomas, 2nd Lord Wharton, another veteran of the Border Wars, represented several parliamentary constituencies from 1545 to 1558 and was buried in Westminster Abbey. Philip, the son who succeeded him in 1572 as 3rd Baron Wharton, entertained James I at Wharton Hall in 1617. Lord Philip Wharton, the 4th Lord, born in 1613, had a long and satisfying life, his death occurring at the age of eighty-three. Six years before he died, he began to distribute Bibles to children who committed to heart certain verses from the Good Book. This work was sustained by the income of his 463-acre estate in Sinningthwaite, Yorkshire. A prominent Puritan statesman and friend of Cromwell, Philip was dubbed 'the Good Lord' Wharton. Thomas, his son, who rose to the rank of Marquis, was an outstanding Whig and author of the words of the song *Lillibulero*, a satire on James II's appointment of a zealous Roman Catholic as Lord Lieutenant of Ireland. It was said that the catchy tune whistled a king out of three kingdoms. Wharton Hall remained in the hands of the family until the sequestration of the estates in the 18th century on the attainder of Philip, Duke of Wharton for high treason.

The Howards of Great Corby, beside the lower Eden, were major landowners. Corby had been the setting for a castle since the 12th century. Two centuries

46 *Sir Richard Salkeld and his wife, as pictured in Wetheral church by S. Harrison, 1898.*

later, in the days of the Salkelds, a pele tower was built. Lord William Howard, third son of the 4th Duke of Norfolk, acquired it for his second son, who added a substantial house capped by a huge sculpted lion which, according to local tradition, wagged its tail at midnight on New Year's Eve. The grounds, which stretch for one and a half miles along the riverside, contain many curious architectural features, including a cascade. Queen Anne remarked to one of the Howards, 'You have a beautiful place at Corby, I hear.' Walter Scott mentioned to the Howards some words about Corby written on the window of the *Bush Inn* at Carlisle in the mid-18th century:

> Here chicks in eggs for breakfast sprawl,
> Here godless boys God's glories squall,
> While rebels' heads adorn the wall;
> But Corby's walks atone for all.

In 1791 a Howard Chapel was built above the mausoleum of the family in Wetheral church. A prominent position was allocated to a marble statue sculpted by Joseph Nollekens (1732-1823) commemorating Maria, wife of Henry Howard, and her baby daughter, both of whom died in November 1789. Maria was 22 years of age. Henry Howard designed the Pugin-influenced church at Warwick Bridge which was opened in 1841.

Early in the 19th century Henry, a keen soldier trained in the Austrian army, raised the Cumberland Rangers, a mixed cavalry and infantry unit. He had been barred from a commission in the British Army because he was a Catholic. His son Philip took a Lord Lieutenant's commission as Captain of the Corby Defence Association Company, which existed for 'the protection of property and preservation of Peace within the Parishes of Wetheral and Warwick'. The cross and steps on Wetheral Green, which was purchased from the Commissioners of the Common of Inglewood, enclosed in 1808, were erected at the expense of the ubiquitous Henry Howard.

47 *The Luck of Edenhall, now in the Victoria and Albert Museum in London.*

Twenty generations of Crackanthorpes lived in Newbiggin Hall, beside the Crowdundle Beck. At the heart of the hall is the obligatory pele tower, although a tower in the narrow Crowdundle valley would have been overlooked by many raiding Scots. Its defence lay less in a dominating position than in the series of moats created by the diversion of the beck. The tower was a ruin when, towards the end of the 15th century, the family built the tower known as Jerusalem. Further building greatly enlarged the hall yet, with the choice of a single type of stone, the house had a unified appearance.

Crackanthorpes lived at Newbiggin until the male line became extinct in the 18th century. Dorothy Crackanthorpe, the heiress of Newbiggin, married William Cookson of Penrith and her descendants took the name and arms of Crackanthorpe. Dorothy and William were to achieve lasting fame as the grandparents of the poet William Wordsworth. A programme of building and repair transformed a house that had been sadly neglected. The work was inspired by Christopher Crackanthorpe Cookson (later Crackanthorpe) and extended over seven years until his death in 1799. He erected a fine coach house, cart house and a stable block facing the hall.

William Crackanthorpe, a kindly and benevolent man who died in 1888 aged 98 years, owned an estate that extended to about 12,000 acres. When the surveyors of the Midland Railway, prospecting for the best route for the Settle-Carlisle line, proposed to fell one of his favourite woods, William asked that a single tree might be spared. The engineers readily agreed but inquired why he wanted to keep the tree. Crackanthorpe replied, 'So I might hang from it the whole Midland Railway board.' Newbiggin Hall and estate passed out of the Crackanthorpe family in 1954.

The Grahams, for long association with Netherby and with the life of north Cumberland, were originally a Scottish family who indulged in Moss Trooping and consequently suffered years of exile in Ireland, where border troublemakers might be sent by Lord Burghley acting on behalf of Queen Elizabeth. The Grahams were among those who crept back. In about 1620 Richard Graham, son of Fergus Graham, who had a smallholding called the Plump, bought Netherby from the Clifford family and transformed a wild, peaty landscape that had been fought over for two centuries so that virtually all that remained standing were pele towers. Netherby's ancient core is a pele.

Richard Graham became Master of the Horse to the Duke of Buckingham, who was Master of the Horse to King James, and was awarded a baronetcy. Dr Robert Graham made a profound visual change at Netherby in the 18th century when he drained and manured the land and set out farms on his large estate. He also built the well-named settlement of Longtown. A considerable part of the Netherby estate was sold about the time of the First World War.

The Faradays are best remembered because of the achievements of one of their sons, Michael Faraday, physical philosopher and inventor of the electric dynamo. His outlook and attitudes rested on the austere and simple faith of his ancestors. The Faradays and Hastwells, who were related through marriage, belonged to a small, despised Christian sect founded on the teachings of Robert Sandeman, a Scotsman whose teaching was based on that of John

48 *William Crackanthorpe, 1877, a landowner affected when the Settle-Carlisle railway was proposed.*

Glas (1695-1773). Michael Faraday's father, James (1761-1810), blacksmith at Outhgill, courted a maidservant called Margaret Hastwell. They were married in June 1786, when James was aged 25 and Margaret three years younger. Weddings in Independent chapels being unlawful, the ceremony took place at Kirkby Stephen parish church.

The Faradays moved to Clapham Wood End, in north-west Yorkshire, worshipping at a Sandemanian meeting house near the River Wenning. Dr James F. Riley, in a Dalesman book entitled *The Hammer and the Anvil* (1954), records that James took his family from Clapham to London in search of a better job. Michael was born here in 1791 and given the Christian name of his Westmorland grandfather. Young Faraday had a modest education, was apprenticed to a bookseller and avidly read scientific books, especially those relating to electricity. His experiments led him to write *Experimental Researches in Electricity* (3 vols, 1839, 1844, 1855).

The knowledge contained in the books radically changed life on earth but Faraday did not forget his humble origins. At the height of his scientific career he was asked by a sculptor to sit for a portrait bust. The sculptor noticed a sudden tenderness on the face of his subject and inquired the reason for it. Said Faraday, 'You dropped your chisel and the sound as it struck the floor reminded me of my childhood. It was the sound of the hammer and the anvil. My father was a smith.'

Chapter 7

Market Towns

arly settlers in the Eden Valley preferred life on the free-draining uplands to the vale, where there was an unhealthy mix of dense forest and cloying swamp. Anglian settlers – the English, that is – were living hereabouts for over a thousand years before they were driven out by the Danes. Appleby, its Danish name meaning 'farmstead with an apple tree', achieved prominence under the Normans. William II granted the Barony of Westmorland to Ranulf de Meschines (or Mesquin), one of his favourite knights, who built the castle that became the focus of the small town.

The durability of that first motte and bailey type castle was tested in 1175 when William the Lion, the Scottish king, and his army arrived unexpectedly. Appleby, being open to the north, was destroyed and the exultant Scots went on to wreak havoc at Brough, further up the Eden Valley. Appleby Castle was strengthened and the settlement rebuilt as a planned community. Extending on either side of the main street were burgage plots occupied by immigrants to the new castle-town. Appleby occupies a gentle slope in a steep-sided loop of the River Eden, which divides the parishes of St Lawrence, a popular dedication in new towns of the 12th century, and St Michael, also known as Bongate, 'where the villeni [tied tenants] stay' (they served the castle).

Bongate was a point where the river was easily forded. Today a footbridge spans it, and lower down a twin-arched bridge leads from the Sands, an area that was rapidly developed in the railway age, into a street that was intentionally narrow, a defensive strategem in troublesome times. Bridge Street gives way to elegant Boroughgate, the layout of which evokes the spirit of a medieval market town. At the head of Boroughgate, massive iron gates in a high wall form the main entrance to Appleby Castle, now thought of primarily as the castle of the Cliffords. They and their descendants, Thanet and Hothfield, held it for centuries until 1962, when it was sold to a private buyer.

At the lower end of the main street, St Lawrence's church is on a site hallowed by Christians since Danish times. Twice burned down by the Scots, the church

49 *Appleby in 1834. Women are drawing water from the Eden.*

was eventually provided with a tower whose stout walls and narrow entrance gave refuge in future raids. The lowest part of the tower dates to the 12th century. The porch was added in about 1300, though dog-tooth moulding is a feature of the arch which could be a century older. The church is approached through cloisters built in 1811, a secondary use of which was to shelter farmers' wives who gathered here on market day to sell butter and eggs.

A lofty, white-painted pillar at each end of Boroughgate marks the limits of the market. The High Cross, near the castle gateway, forms a useful traffic island. The Low Cross embellishes the Market Place. Appleby received its first market charter in 1174, the income of the town being largely derived from tolls and the rents charged for stalls. The start of trading is marked by the ringing of a bell. The Mayor and Council meet in an ancient Moot Hall, a *moot* being a term for a meeting. Special meetings were called whenever there were disputes over, for example, short measures in the market. Some of the old measures, for bushels and pecks, survive. The Moot Hall housed the Assize Courts until 1770.

William de Goldington became the first mayor in 1265. The town treasures the original borough seal. Other cherished items include the mayoral jewel and chain, and a splendid early 18th-century mace. A silver loving-cup dated 1703 is passed round at the Mayoral Retiring Dinner. The toast is 'Appleby-in-Westmorland, root and branch; may it flourish for ever.' Henry II granted the burgesses of Appleby generous privileges. His charter was extended in 1212 by King John, who bestowed on the burgesses control of local government and freedom from feudal impositions. Appleby prospered, having a mayor and two provosts.

The Scots, buoyed up by their success against the English at Bannockburn, swept through the Eden Valley again, putting Appleby to the torch. On St Stephen's Day 1388, a surprise attack by the Scots caused so much damage that as late as 1515 the town was reported to be 'greatly diminished and fallen into ruin'. The coat of arms adopted by Appleby features the salamander, a creature reputed to be able to live in fire, which is an allusion to the 1388 attack. Dragons recall the ancient British kingdom of Cumbria. The town's motto is 'Neither by sword nor by fire'.

Plague ravaged the townsfolk in 1598. In the Civil War the burghers of Appleby, loyal to the King, were gravely affected when Parliament introduced a new restraining charter. As the document arrived in town, the mayor withdrew and the bailiffs resigned their offices rather than make the proclamation. The Revd Thomas Machell recorded that the Roundhead soldiery found in the market a Kirkby Stephen man, who 'proclaimed it aloud, while the people stopped their ears and hearts, having nothing upon but their eyes and those ever filled with tears'. The charter was annulled on the Restoration of the Monarchy, the Restoration mayor in 1660 delaying taking the oath or receiving the staff of authority until he was provided with scissors with which to cut into pieces the sheepskin of the charter.

After Lady Anne Clifford inherited the family estates in Craven and Westmorland, Appleby became to her 'the most auntient Seate of mine inheritance'. She occupied her northern estates at a time when the properties were dilapidated but between 1651 and 1658 she set the remedial work in progress. The castle had been ruined since 1569 but was defended during the Civil Wars. Surrendered in 1648, the building was slighted and Lady Anne restored it, despite the edict that such a thing should never happen. In 1651 a small army of masons, joiners and lead-beaters worked on the tower, fitting new floors, raising the roof to 80 feet and giving it a coverlet of lead. Her ladyship now had a viewpoint from which to survey her much-loved Pennine panorama. Anne restored St Lawrence's church and rebuilt St Michael's.

Boroughgate is flanked by some notable buildings. The rather plain façade of Lady Anne's almshouses conceals a picturesque cobbled courtyard around which the houses and a chapel are arranged. Splendid houses include the White

House, built for John Robinson and originally painted yellow in deference to the Lowther family, who assisted him during his rise to fame. A politician who served in Lord North's ministry of 1770-82, Robinson was fickle in his allegiances, prompting a fellow Member of Parliament in a heated moment to make what became a celebrated remark: 'Before I could say Jack Robinson.' Until recent times the White House was the home of a doctor, Peter Delap, who described Robinson to me as a 'Mr Fixit' of his time.

The original county gaol, a mean structure, was situated at the West End of the old bridge, having formerly been a private chapel dedicated to St John the Baptist. Two men, inspired by the preaching of George Fox, were among the early Quakers imprisoned here: James Naylor, who had become a travelling speaker, was arrested for preaching unsound doctrine; Francis Howgill's crime was preaching in the street. Their trial probably took place when the Sessions were held in the Moot Hall in January 1653, and they were committed to the local gaol for five months. A consequence of the trial was that Anthony Pearson, one of the

50 *A composite picture of Lady Anne's Almshouses, Appleby, in 1967. A Mother presided over the elderly ladies who were known as Sisters.*

presiding judges who denounced Quakerism, sought out George Fox for his own good, being 'afraid lest the orders we made at Appleby cause some to suffer, who speak from the mouth of the Lord; I heartily wish they were suppressed or recalled.'

Francis Howgill died in captivity in Appleby, aged 50, in 1669. In the early days of his imprisonment he wrote, 'People are so made [sic] and rude hereabouts I can hardly either receive a letter or write one. I have so bad a jailer, who is very often the cause of detaining any stranger and getting them into bonds for his gain, insomuch that I am sometimes more troubled for them than for myself. Of late he will let none speak with me.' He found contentment in his final years and was permitted to have visitors. Among his good friends was the gaoler who had tormented him. A new gaol, built in 1771, was hidden from the outer world by a high-walled courtyard. The energy of the inmates was absorbed by a treadmill, on which grain was ground, young delinquents being taught reading and writing.

Appleby Grammar School was built in 1887 to replace an old school situated in Low Wiend, near the church. Queen Elizabeth granted letters of incorporation for this school in 1574. Anciently, the Barony of Appleby became the county town of Westmorland, but this status was lost with the boundary changes of 1974, when Westmorland was absorbed in the new county of Cumbria. The county offices are in Carlisle so the proud citizens of Appleby, aware of their heritage, changed the name of the town to Appleby-in-Westmorland.

Appleby and Kirkby Stephen are as chalk and cheese. Proud Kirkby, market town of the upper dale, has not had the patronage of a castle-based aristocracy, though Norman blood flowed through the veins of families with estates in the district. William T. Palmer, writing about the two towns just before the Second World War led to major social changes, commented, 'In politics, they as a rule favour different parties. I am told that Appleby is naturally Tory in outlook and Kirkby Stephen is out to make experiments to obtain a better social structure than the present.'

Kirkby Stephen, the highest town in the Eden Valley, lies at 570 feet above sea level. Alfred Wainwright, travelling on the Settle-Carlisle train which runs on a ledge high above the town and about two miles from the centre, commented on the landscape change, from the 'white flashes of limestone' to 'the rich red of sandstone'. The population of around 2,000 people swells enormously in summer when tourists in cars and coaches stop here for rest and refreshment. Most of the buildings have a view of the impressively long main street that changes its name several times from one end to the other.

Buildings that have not been colour-washed have a rosy appearance from the local stone of which they are built. This is 'brockram', red sandstone flecked with pieces of limestone which is quarried in a gorge to the east of the town. Gordon Wood left a vivid picture of the gorge: 'Here the pink slabs of 'brockram' have been repeatedly submerged by countless floods down the narrow gorge. When the river is low, great potholes, eroded by milling pebbles, are exposed to view … At one place the whole river plunges down a crevice that a foot-rule would span. A local story tells how a blacksmith with a mighty fist did indeed once bridge the river between thumb and little finger. The River Eden, infused by local becks, is seen by those who take a short walk from the market place to Frank's Bridge.'

The church, proudly known as 'the Cathedral of the Dale' because of its size, has a 70ft tower that demands to be noticed. The building is approached through elegant cloisters. The Truppstone, a flat-topped tombstone standing in grand isolation now that the other tombstones have been moved to create a green space, is said to be associated with the Whartons. Generations of Kirkby Stephen folk visited the stone on Easter Monday and left money in payment of the Vicar's Tithes.

The town's name is derived from the Norse *kirk* and *bye* (church town). Much speculation has surrounded the name Stephen. It is unusual for a town to be named after a saint, and R.R. Sowerby, a local historian, theorised that the Stephen who is patron of the church might have been no more than 'a chieftain of early times'. The Revd A.N. Rigg, a former vicar, linked Stephen with an abbot of St Mary's at York who received the church from one Ivo Taillebois. The Saxon church was rebuilt at

51 *Aspects of Kirkby Stephen. The drawing entitled 'Satan in Bonds' show the Locki Stone preserved in the parish church.*

the end of the 12th century, and in about 1500 a high tower succeeded one of Early English style that was semi-ruined. Not far from the main entrance to the church is a prominently displayed piece from an Anglo-Danish cross shaft featuring Loki, a Norse god, in the form of a bound devil.

A writer in the *Gentleman's Magazine* in the mid-18th century commented on the Monday market, at which stocking manufacture was the main trade: 'This traffic is the first at the market; it generally begins about six, and is over about eight in the morning. Tho' the situation of Kirkby Stephen is under bleak and barren mountains, yet the communication with several of their own dales, and with Yorkshire, along the river heads, affords a pretty considerable market, an advantage that Brough near Stainmore has now lost for want of such connection.' The stockings were hand-knitted from worsted distributed by hosiers who then collected the finished products. The folk of Ravenstonedale – women, men, even children – excelled at stocking production, the output at its peak being 1,000 pairs a week. Sowerby wrote, 'The stockings were conveyed to the towns and other centres where required by pack-horses over the numerous bridle-paths.'

Nonconformity in its various forms made a mark on local life and by the mid-19th century the temperance movement had strong support in the Eden Valley. At Kirkby Stephen this led, in 1856, to the construction of a Temperance Hall of a vaguely classical style with, above the main door, the now flaking figure of a lady clothed in blue. For a time, the town was reputed to have more places of worship than public houses. William T. Palmer, a visitor in the inter-war years, wrote that the townsfolk had

> dabbled in every kind of Nonconformity … it has enjoyed revivals, started meetings and classes and congregations of all sorts, of which relics of chapels, meeting houses and presumably 'isolated members' still remain … George Fox, George Whitehead, John Wesley, and all the other society makers seem to have reached Kirkby Stephen in their turn … In addition, every hamlet round this head of the Eden seems to have chapel if not church, and Sunday School.

Among the 'local characters' was John Fawcett, who drove the mail gig between Kirkby Stephen and Tebay. He owned three horses and each animal had two days' rest between journeys. In winter, John was so swaddled in clothes he could scarcely be seen. He had a heavy whip and a revolver to protect the mail. After collecting it from Kirkby Stephen, he drove to Ravenstonedale and Newbiggin for their letters, then went on to Tebay, returning to Kirkby about 2 a.m. the next day. He was never known to climb down from his gig and the postmen who met him handled the mail.

Long before John Fawcett took to the road, a postal scandal rocked Kirkby Stephen. Early in the 19th century the poet William Wordsworth was responsible for the distribution of postage stamps in Westmorland. John Hall of Kirkby Stephen, a sub-distributor, had not recorded in his returns almost £300 from legacy receipts, and Wordsworth travelled to the town, seized Hall's movable goods, and by selling them met the shortfall. The luckless Hall was arrested and found guilty of larceny.

Chapter 8

Fairs and Festivals

Carlisle evolved as a market town in the Middle Ages, the main fair being held on the Feast of the Assumption of the Blessed Virgin Mary (15 August). Extending over 15 days, it stimulated trade and the city benefited from the stallage, or tolls levied on goods brought for sale. Joyce and Brian Blake, in their story of Carlisle, published when the city was celebrating its 800th birthday in 1958, harked back to the 1870s and '80s. Carlisle then 'was one big noisy market'. Traders were to be found in all the streets within the walls of the ancient town. The Sands served as a reception centre for Irish cattle and the celebrated black cattle of Galloway; pigs were marketed in Solway Terrace, near Eden Bridge, and the market for horses, pigs and poultry took place in Lowther Street. The Corn Market was actually in the middle of English Street and Green Market lived up to its name, being the place where vegetables were sold. Quality potatoes were on offer in Castle Street.

Fairs gave up-country farmers the chance to dispose of their surplus livestock before the onset of winter. This was especially true of Luke Fair, which took place at Kirkby Stephen in October. Immense numbers of sheep and cattle were offered for sale, the sheep being held in pens belonging to the owners of shops and house frontages and rented out to visiting farmers. Cattle stood in the Market Square and in North Road. R.R. Sowerby, who lived at Winton, described Luke Fair as a great meeting place for dale-country sheep farmers and recorded the sort of conversation that might be heard on market day: 'Hoo is ter?' 'Oh, ah's gayly, hoo's thee sel?' 'What sec a trade hes ter hed?' 'Ah've selt twee or three ord teups [tups] gay weel, but t'yows are worth nowt.' Some potential buyers were supplied with strong drink at the nearest inn. There was a saying that 'a drink or two's a grand thing fer lousenen purse strings.'

King John instituted a Saturday market at Appleby for corn and all kinds of provisions and the market is still a feature of local life. Until 1885 various fairs, including the event on St Lawrence's Day, 21 August, were 'walked' by the Mayor and Corporation. A proclamation was read at the High Cross near the Castle

52 *Clock Tower at Brough, a village with an ancient fair that is now by-passed by the Stainmore Road.*

Gate, at the *Grapes Inn*, on The Sands, and then at the *King's Head*, where the company dined on bread, cheese and short cake washed down by ale.

King John also granted Kirkoswald a charter for a weekly market and an annual fair, to be held on 5 August (St Oswald's Day). The village of Brough in the upper Eden Valley had a fair from about the same time, and the profit in 1280 amounted to ten shillings. The celebrated Brough Hill Fair was originally established by a charter granted to Robert de Clifford by Edward III in 1329. The original venue, Brough Intack, was changed to the Hill in about 1661 following an outbreak of plague. The Brough Hill Fair, held on a bleak, exposed area adjacent to the Appleby-Bowes main road, was on 21 September, the feast of St Matthew, and the following day. The dates were subsequently changed to 30 September and 1 October. The fair had a reputation for wind and rain.

Brough Hill burgeoned after 1752 with the growth of cattle-droving from Scotland. The season began in May and reached its peak in the autumn, and by the early part of the 19th century, when cattle and sheep as well as horses were changing hands, it was rated as one of the largest fairs in the north country. Crayston Webster, an authority on 19th-century Westmorland, commented that the 'considerable quantities of Galloway, Highland, Irish and Dutch cattle ... shown at the great fairs of Appleby and Brough ... spreading through the country, led to crosses with the shorthorns, which raised useful stock for the high-lying farms'. When, in 1865, an outbreak of the contagious disease known as rinderpest affected cattle fairs, Brough Hill escaped closure but saw restricted trade.

Jonty Wilson, blacksmith at Kirkby Lonsdale for many years and a considerable horseman, told me that a man who bought a horse from one of the sharp-witted travellers at Brough Hill should have experienced every trick in the book or he would be 'diddled'. J.D. Marshall, writing in *Cumbria* magazine, mentioned the 'horse-coper', one of whose specialities was dealing in 'long-tailed staggs', or young horses. 'The work of haltering these young animals, which had never previously had a halter upon their heads, was a striking spectacle. When a buyer singled one out, a young man 'more developed physically than mentally' would catch the horse in question.'

Some men became drovers as well as graziers. The fair encouraged people to borrow money and to travel and develop a commercial sense. In some cases such indulgence led to financial ruin. In later years Brough Hill Fair was patronised mainly by travelling folk. Tom Barbour, a young constable in October 1927, joined seven constables and a sergeant for a four-day spell of duty at the fair. On the opening day, a steady stream of caravans ranged in appearance from the immaculate and well-painted hooped vans to modern caravans, most of which were well-kept. There were also flat carts with canvas covers for shelter, each attended by numerous children. The retinue of haltered horses varied in age, size and colour. As each family of travellers arrived, it received a rapturous welcome from kinsfolk.

Stalls were erected and side-shows and a small circus arrived. At the height of the fair, a cacophony of cries arose from smallholders and cheapjacks. Cheap meals, mainly hot pies and peas, were provided. The police did not intervene in the noisy, inter-group quarrels, and if a bare-knuckle fight broke out the two protagonists stripped to the waist. The bout was usually savage but fair, ending with a handshake. The travelling folk lived, up to a point, off the land: Tom Barbour intercepted a man carrying a live hedgehog which he intended to kill, cook and eat. It would taste like chicken – but with more flavour.

Animals driven in from a wide area included farm horses, light horses and ponies. Tom remembered when a drove of fell ponies was herded away from the rest, the huddled animals wild-eyed with fear. Elsewhere, a youth would run a horse through a corridor of critical spectators several times, before one of them stepped forward and flicked the animal with his whip to indicate that he was interested. The owner of the animal would walk towards him, loudly extolling the qualities of the pony. The two men, having haggled and fixed a price, smacked each other's hand to seal the deal.

For some of the young people it was a time for romance, a surreptitious courtship begun at the New Fair at Appleby continuing at Brough. On a dark evening, when large stick fires were lit and melodeons played, amorous couples drifted away

53 *Travellers and their mounts in a composite drawing of Appleby New Fair.*

from the crowds. Silvester Gordon Boswell related that parents disliked this type of behaviour and elopements were fairly common. In due course, marriages between travellers conformed with those in ordinary society, those arranged at Brough being quietly solemnised at Penrith Registry Office.

Brough Hill Fair began to decline with the opening of the Eden Valley railway. A writer observed in the *Westmorland Gazette* on 7 October 1865 that local people might now shift their cattle by rail. William T. Palmer wrily commented in print, 'The ancients used to declare that the railways reduced the entries at the Fair – but they only remembered the record years when droves of horses pastured all the way to Brough and Appleby and black cattle were turned out on the commons at Brackenber to feed where they could find grass. They did not recall the years of black disaster, of rinderpest, foot-and-mouth and pleuro-pneumonia [*sic*] when the Hill was almost deserted.' After 1941 the fair was held courtesy of the War Department, who had purchased a vast tract of the district as a tank training area.

Appleby Fair received its charter from James II in June 1685. The name New Fair came into use when the Gregorian Calendar was established in 1752, and the traditional dates for the fair are the second Wednesday in June and the day preceding. The timetable is less predictable than it was, with travelling folk varying their time of arrival and departure. 'Travellers' converging on the domed 32-acre Fair Hill (formerly Gallows Hill) in early June have long outnumbered those reared in strict Romany traditions, and most arrive in motor vehicles towing large caravans, although some adopt the traditional hooped wagons of their forebears, which are still drawn by horses – piebalds for preference. The journey takes several days. At night, the horses are drawn off the road and staked out to graze the verges while meals are cooked.

The fame of this event has rested mainly on horse dealing which is, however, not referred to in the charter. Celebrity animals, known as 'gipsy cobs', might be black and white or brown and white. A crowd gathered on Appleby Bridge watches trotters and pacers being driven into the

54   *Silvester Gordon Boswell, a traveller associated with Appleby New Fair for many years.*

water to have their legs washed – an action that might add £100 to the value of a good horse – before they are groomed on the Sands, a stretch of low riverside ground. The aforementioned Silvester Gordon Boswell, a senior traveller and owner of a thriving scrapyard at Spalding, first visited the fair with his father before the First World War, and related that in the early 1920s up to a hundred Irish horses were on show in Boroughgate, the heart of the town. The appearance of Model T Ford cars – the 'Tin Lizzies' – scared the unbroken colts, which were moved from the main road to a secluded place beyond the railway viaduct.

Attempts were made in the mid-1960s to have the fair closed down. A reprieve was granted following pressure from some influential people, including a member of the Lowther family. Gallows Hill came available at modest charge, and was provided with a piped water supply and latrines. When I first visited Appleby New Fair in 1964, the streets of the little town held a concourse of cars, vans, lorries and horse-drawn carts driven by travellers whose faces radiated pride and pleasure. Cigar-smoking men handling wads of banknotes with a casual air were invading the shops, and in the cafes ample helpings of fish, eggs, peas and chips were being tucked away.

Caravans stretched in long, almost unbroken, lines by the roadside towards Long Marton. The hooped wagons were blurred to the sight by blue smoke rising from camp fires and the contents of the travellers' vans were exposed to popular gaze, for on show days every status symbol, including the best china, was on

55 *Travelling folk at Appleby (with the author on the left). Precious collections of Crown Derby were displayed in the modern caravans.*

show. Crown Derby was especially prized for its colour. A proud owner said, 'We are little Egyptians; we don't like white. Crown Derby is pretty, colourful and decorative.' It was bought both to display and as an investment.

Travellers wore their best clothes. A family from Shelf, near Bradford, had travelled by horse and hooped caravan via Harrogate and Borougbridge, leaving the Great North Road at Scotch Corner and crossing Stainmore to the Eden Valley. This was thought to be easier for the horses than a direct route over Buckhaw Brow, near Settle, and the Shap Fells. Parked nearby, in modern trailers, were four daughters and two sons, with their families. The Irish visitors were most distinctive. A gnarled old woman sitting beside a camp fire smoked a clay pipe as she listened to the song of a canary, the bird's cage dangling from the branch of a tree.

Joe Gatenby, a traveller from Bradford who first attended the New Fair in 1919, remembered the post-war slump during which prices for good animals ranged from £7 to £50. A blacksmith charged 5s. for shoeing a carthorse. No charge was made for attending to a donkey. In 1964 Clive Holroyd of Kippax, one of several blacksmiths, heated horseshoes made of mild steel in a flaming jet of propane gas. As he slotted a hot shoe into place on the hoof of a horse, there was a whiff of frizzled horn and the air clouded with acrid smoke.

56 *A traveller on a light horse-drawn cart shows it off along the Sands at Appleby.*

57 *Trotting a horse displays its good points to potential buyers at Appleby New Fair.*

58 *Detail from the rich and ornate patterning on a traveller's van.*

Strident voices – 'oy, oy, oy' – might be heard above the sound of pounding hooves as horses were displayed before potential buyers. The action of running a horse up and down created excitement, and after several runs the horse was halted, a small crowd gathered and bidding began. Within ten minutes, the price might climb so rapidly that the still perspiring horse had changed hands three or four times. A fat roll of money was produced in a deal that ended with a hand-slap. In the event of a disagreement over a horse, an older man would emerge from the crowd, stand between the two protagonists, hand on the shoulder of each, and through quiet talking end the dispute by splitting the difference in price. This would be followed by the resounding hand-slap. The arbitrator was akin to the 'tangler' of the small towns of Old Ireland where cattle were traded in the streets, and like the 'tangler' he would probably be paid for his service at the conclusion of the deal.

The New Fair I first toured had virtually every breed of horse and pony, a goat, terriers, lurchers, scores of dark-haired men, onlookers like myself and one or two good-natured policemen. In 1970 it took place in a drought and there was a turnover of about a thousand horses. Three thousand people thronged Fair Hill, on which had assembled around 600 trailers, attendant lorries and cars, and some horse-drawn wagons – about 2,400 units in all. That year, alas, the Hill erupted in violence as a quarrel between families was resolved.

59 *A finely decorated cart of the type used by travelling folk.*

60 *Horses on parade at Appleby.*

On the Northern Pennines, Alston Fair was a major attraction. Martha James (1846-1932), a novelist who used the *nom-de-plume* Austin Clare, left us descriptions of the fair in her novel *Davie Armstrong*. The event was attended by 'grey plaided shepherds and herdsmen' who 'drove their horned sheep and shaggy hornless black cattle up the narrow street leading to the Fair Hill'. They shouted and hallooed at the top of their voices. Women with baskets sat on 'the dilapidated steps of the old market cross which, by the way, is not a cross at all but a very tumbledown roof, supported on eight time-worn pillars and surmounted by a gas lamp'. On all sides were temporary stalls holding 'wooden dairy utensils, oranges and apples, gingerbread horses of a peculiar species unknown to naturalists, sticks of toffee, gorgeously painted sugar candy and nondescript goods of every sort. Here some men were putting up a wooden peep-show; there a Cheap Jack was perched in front of his travelling wagon, filling the air with cries of "Who'll buy? Who'll buy? The most beautiful mirror ever made, fit to reflect your bonny faces my winsome lasses. Dirt cheap."'

Almost three centuries ago, the village of Langwathby in the Eden Valley was famed for 'a fair stone bridge' (now a bailey bridge) and for 'a horse course over its moor'. The races, which began in the reign of Henry VIII, had become so well-known during the reign of Elizabeth I they were attended by people from both the English and Scottish sides of the border. The notorious Kinmont Willie – he who escaped from Carlisle Castle – attended this and other meetings. The sale of English horses to the Scots, though strictly forbidden, took place surreptitiously. Langwathby races were last held towards the end of the 18th century. Mary Powley, last of the old school of Cumberland dialect poets, knew the village well enough to lament its decline:

> But thou, whom fairy never haunted,
> Nor grimmer ghost or goblin daunted,
> No light of giant, seer, or sage
> Reflects on thy dull after-age.
> No castle, cave, or Druid spot –
> All but thy name appears forgot.

Thomas Sandford wrote a perplexing account of a great match on the 'famous horse course' at Langanby Moor (*sic*) between the Earl of Moray's 'wily horse Fox' and an English horse called Conqueror; it is perplexing because it appears in a confused medley of events including the writer's relief at the death of Cromwell. Conqueror triumphed and won the money, 'though the night before ther was the terriblest blast ever blown; churches, towers, trees, steeples, houses all feling the furie of the furies thereof. The devil a stir whether of England or Scotland I cannot tell, but the English horse got the prise. The great stores of woods was so blowen done across the waye as we had much adoe to ride thorow them, yet not so bad a blast as usurping Oliver had when the devil blew him out of this world, God knows whither.' Most of the moor on which the horse races took place was broken up for cultivation in the mid-19th century. The last piece, of about three acres, was ploughed out during the Second World War.

Many Eden Valley villages have their annual fetes, sports or festivals. There is a gala mood at Warcop when the Rushbearing takes place. Historically, rushes were gathered annually to replace the previous year's rushes and strewn on the earthen floor of churches, supposedly to sweeten them. Another theory is that they were intended to keep the feet of worshippers warm in winter. The Warcop Rushbearing, which I viewed on St Peter's Day 1963, turned out to be one of those colourful but undramatic events suiting the temperament of the valley folk. How St Peter became associated with the church at Warcop is not known, since the local church is dedicated to St Columba.

At two o'clock, men carried the small, hand-embroidered banner of St Peter to the centre of the road and a military band, transported from Catterick by bus, formed up behind. (Through the purchase of Warcop Hall, the Army had become lord of the manor. The hall was re-sold but the manorial rights stayed with the Crown, ownership of a vast firing range making it by far the largest landowner in the parish.) Children were marshalled into line. Girls clad in brightly coloured frocks and jumpers held on their heads floral crowns that had been built on wooden frames. Boys, who were only admitted to the proceedings as recently as the 1930s, carried crosses made of rushes.

The procession moved slowly through the straggling village. At Warcop Hall the Army had provided lemonade and biscuits for the children, to be consumed at leisure while the perspiring bandsmen continued to play. From the hall it was a short journey to St Columba's church, where the service was an abbreviated Evensong, including a Rushbearing hymn. The congregation occupied 18th-century box pews under Warcop's magnificent 15th-century collarbeam roof. Children presented their crowns and crosses, which were temporarily stacked round the altar. They would then be hung over the church's main door for almost a year, until the bases of the crowns were needed for another Rushbearing.

Chapter 9

Religious Witness

The Britons reverenced various gods, as well as natural features such as rivers and hills. In Roman times, respect for the Emperor was demanded but local gods were tolerated and so temples abounded. Tullie House, at Carlisle, has an impressive collection of inscribed Roman stones (see fig. 20). A tombstone to the memory of Vacia, an infant aged three, has a carving of a female in a belted tunic and cloak. The destructive power of death is symbolised on a woman's gravestone by a winged sphinx holding a skull and two lions devouring human heads. The woman holds a fan and her son is touching a pet bird that reposes on her lap.

An altar to Jupiter was filched during the construction of Lanercost Priory in a quiet valley near Brampton. On a visit to Lanercost in 1966 I was taken into the *cellarium*, where several Roman altars are stored for safe-keeping, included one raised to Cocidius (a local god of war) and another to Silvanus (god of the woods). Britons who lived in Roman towns or in settlements along Hadrian's Wall doubtless worshipped deities that had affinities with their own gods. Converts introduced Christianity to *Luguvalium* (Carlisle), and early in the third century the worship of Christ was formalised. The Emperor Constantine ordered that 'complete toleration should be given by the state to anyone who had given up his mind either to the cult of the Christians or to any other cult which he personally feels best for himself'.

Abandoned by the Romans, the Britons divided themselves into small kingdoms, that of Rheged being based on Carlisle. Coelhen, the first recorded king, is the Old King Cole of the nursery rhymes. Sometime about AD 573, St Kentigern, apparently on a mission from the Celtic church in Glasgow, preached at 'Crosfeld', or Crosthwaite, near Keswick. He became a cult figure after whom a number of Cumbrian churches would be named. The Christian church thus survived the Roman withdrawal and before long other Celtic missionaries from the north were active. They were dubbed 'saints', not through formal recognition but because their holy, selfless manner and witness were saintly. Initially they preached in the open air, and would have had to compete with many established beliefs.

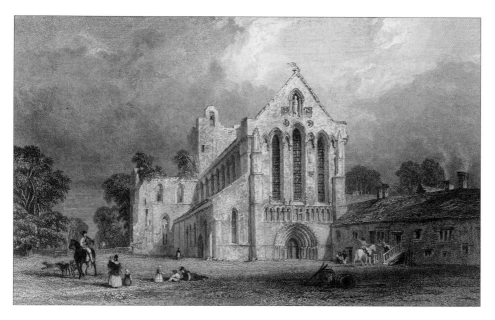

61 *Lanercost Priory, in the Irthing Valley of North Cumberland.*

Godly men who spread Christianity in Cumbria included St Ninian (*c*.360-432). When Carlisle was part of Northumbria, Egfrith, anxious to include Cumberland in his kingdom and unite it within a common church, asked the ageing St Cuthbert to leave his monastery on the Farne Islands and become Bishop of Lindisfarne, with the care of the whole of what is now Cumbria. Visiting Carlisle in 686, Cuthbert was shown a well-established monastery and was impressed by the remnants of Roman masonry, especially a water fountain. Bede records that St Herbert, whose hermitage was situated on an island in Derwentwater, venerated Cuthbert, and each year the two friends met in Carlisle. When, in 687, Cuthbert had a presentiment of his death, he asked his friend to pray they would die at the same time. The prayer was answered and the deaths came to pass on 19 March.

Stone crosses evoke the spirit of the time, their richly carved symbols embodying both Celtic and Anglian ideas. At Bewcastle, a cross dating from early in the seventh century stands over 14 feet high. Originally it would have had a crosshead and been painted in bright colours. Fragments of crosses, providing evidence of an early Christian presence, exist in churches at Dacre and Kirkby Stephen. An Anglo-Saxon tower at the west end of St Laurence's church, Morland would have been known to Edward I, who in October 1292 stayed overnight in the village while on his way from Appleby and Brougham. Norse settlers from Ireland, Scotland and the Isle of Man who found acceptable quarters in Cumbria after

62   *Brough church, with the castle beyond. The castle was built on the site of a Roman fort.*

63   *St Michael's church and Appleby Castle, from* Pennant's Tour.

64 *Arthuret church, about which tales of King Arthur and his Knights are told.*

900 were christianised. In 883 the Abbot of Carlisle enthroned Guthfrith, a Christian who was also the Danish king of Northumbria. Henry I gave lands at Linstock and Carleton to a priest called Walter for the construction and support of a new church at Carlisle, which was established in 1122 or 1123. The community of 26 Augustinian canons, also known as the Black Canons after their garb, were members of a small but dedicated monastic order.

Alston, in the valley of the South Tyne, entered into the ecclesiastical record some time between 1154 and 1189, when Henry II appointed Galfric as Rector. In 1133 Archbishop Thurstan of York detached north-western England from Glasgow, creating a separate bishopric based on Carlisle. Cumberland was classed as a poor area, so Aethelwold, Prior of Nostell in Yorkshire and the first bishop, was allowed to retain his priorate. He died in 1156. The small Norman church existed until early in the 13th century, when the choir was rebuilt in the elegant new Early English style. Those who built the Augustinian priory of Lanercost between 1166 and 1220 used a section of the Roman Wall as a handy quarry. At its nearest point, the Wall was half a mile away and at a higher elevation, so redstone from the west of Lanercost and greys from the east could be sledded to the sacred site.

The streets of Carlisle were trodden by grey-clothed Franciscans, who were housed within the city walls, and Dominicans, known as Black Friars, who moved to quarters within the walls in 1237. The last-named entertained Edward I when he visited Carlisle concerned over the Scottish problem. Ralph Irton, a masterful man who was appointed Bishop in 1280, summoned a synod of the clergy, bullying them into providing contributions for the completion of the cathedral choir. He died in 1292, fatigued after journeying from Parliament in London. That same year the new choir perished in a fire believed to have originated when a young man set fire to his father's house close to the west end of the building and caused immense damage to the city.

Edward I, on a return visit with his nobles and high officers of the Church, doubtless contributed to the cost of rebuilding the cathedral. Robert the Bruce knelt in the blackened remains in 1297, swearing fealty to Edward on the sword of Thomas a Becket. In 1307 the Scottish leader was excommunicated, being cursed in terrible wise with the ringing of bells and burning of candles. The weary Edward offered up his litter in the cathedral before travelling northwards with his army. Edward II, an incompetent ruler, lost the Battle of Bannockburn, which enabled the Scots to resume their raids into northern England. Edward III sojourned with the Franciscans at Christmastide 1332 and the work of renewing the cathedral fabric continued. Fire intervened again in 1392 destroying some of the work.

The Dissolution of the Monasteries from 1536 led to the transfer of property and lands to the Crown. The latter days of the monks at Lanercost were quiet but economically depressing. Having sold off land to meet debts, their income had fallen to below £80 a year when Lord Dacre acquired Lanercost. At the big monasteries, local communities were doubtless saddened at the loss of monastic poor relief and schooling, and travellers no longer had monastic guesthouses at which to lodge and dine. But the expulsion of monks and nuns was not callous, and pensions were available: at Holm Cultram, by the Solway, awards that depended on length of service ranged in value from £2 to £6 per annum.

The heads of monasteries often managed to remain living where they were, with a change of occupation. Lancelot Salkeld, the last Prior of Carlisle, became the first Dean. The Dean and Chapter of Carlisle were granted the monastic possessions of Carlisle and Wetheral. As Henry VIII's commissioners began the work of closing the monasteries, Robert Aske, a Yorkshire lawyer, whipped up opposition for a rebellion that became known as the Pilgrimage of Grace. Men from Brough and Kirkby Stephen converged on Penrith, linking up with Sir Edward Musgrave and his supporters from Edenhall. Eventually a host of people thousands strong marched on Carlisle, where the gates were closed on them. Popular discontent with the Dissolution remained strong. A second rising in February 1537 began in Kirkby Stephen and Appleby, spreading to Penrith and elsewhere, but being leaderless the pilgrims were easily dispersed by the forces of Sir Christopher Dacre. Terrible retribution was exacted. The bodies of luckless men hung in chains at various places throughout the district. It was a grim warning to others.

The Scots captured Carlisle in 1645 and General Leslie ordered the destruction of the cloisters and chapter house. He also claimed all but 40 feet of the nave, needing the stone to repair the city's fortifications. In the 17th century the cathedral was described as being 'black but comely', and 'more like a great wild country church'. For a while in the following century it was a prison, housing Scottish captives after the failure of the 1745 rebellion. After they left, the church was declared 'most nasty' and 'not fit for service for a long while'. In 1764 restoration work was put in hand but repairs to the ceiling were to cost no more than £460. The timbers being rotten, local tradesmen Benjamin Railton and Samuel Halton, joiners, and John Raine, plasterer, were engaged to make a plaster ceiling lower than the timber one and completely hide it.

The spoliation of the cathedral was rectified during the period 1853 to 1857, when what the Dean termed

65   *Outhgill church, in Mallerstang.*

'that noble waggon-shaped roof which the hand of time has greatly defaced' was restored. Sir Walter Scott had been married here on 24 December 1797. The ceremony took place in St Mary's church, a west-end adjunct of the cathedral approached by a separate door.

Edenvale churches acquired many features and objects worthy of a second glance. At St Lawrence's, Appleby, an organ donated by Bishop Smith of Carlisle, once vicar at Appleby, was installed in 1674. Although reputed to be a 'Father Smith', one of the few instruments from the hands of the celebrated organ-builder, it has parts said to be much older, perhaps even connected with the self-same instrument mentioned in the inventory of Carlisle Cathedral in 1571. Dudley Hoys, a well-known Lakeland writer, describing St Lawrence's church in 1961,

THIS CHAPPLE OF MALLERSTANG, AFTER ITT HAD LAYNE RUINOUS AND DECAYED SOME 50 OR 60 YEARS, WAS NEWE REPAYRED BY THE LADY ANNE CLIFFORD, COUNTESSE DOWAGER OF PENBROKE, DORSETT & MONTGOMERY IN THE YEAR 1663, WHO ALLSOE ENDOWED THE SAME WITH LANDS WHICH SHE PURCHASED IN GAWTLEY, NEAR SEDBERGH, TO THE YEARLY VALUE OF ELEAVEN POUNDS FOR EVER. ISAIAH CHAP 58 VER 12. GODS NAME BE PRAISED.

66 *An inscription relating to the restoration of Outhgill church by Lady Anne Clifford.*

related the story of the organ's belonging to the town and not to St Lawrence's, and added, 'Whatever its ancestry and ownership, its tone has a quality to make the listener forget everything but beauty. Mellow, affectionate, it floats through the quietness.'

At Alston, in 1770, there was rejoicing when a new church was opened. Built to a plan drawn up by Smeaton, whose best-known creation was the Eddystone Lighthouse, it replaced a church demolished six years after the Archdeacon of Newcastle, on his visitation of 1763, found the fabric in a bad state. An incongruous but fascinating feature of the present Alston church is a clock it received in 1767 from the Commissioners of Greenwich Hospital. They had acquired it when the Crown awarded them the estates of the Earl of Derwentwater who, having been accused of treason, was beheaded in 1764. The Alston church accounts record the receipt of bell and clock. The bell was duly installed in the new church and, subsequently, in the succeeding church of 1869, where it is still rung daily. Its face having been lost, the clock lay neglected in odd corners for two centuries until, in 1977, funds were raised and it was restored by William Potts & Sons of Leeds.

The musty atmosphere of old-time religion was shaken up in the 17th century by the fresh breeze of new ideas under the general heading of nonconformity. A number of early Quakers languished for a time in Carlisle gaol and John Wesley preached at Carlisle Cross in 1770. By the 19th century Methodism had an impressive base in Carlisle and chapels proliferated in the Eden Valley. Chapel life appealed to the common people, offering them the certainty of faith in Christianity, as well as social life and, in many places, educational facilities. An active part in Methodist services was played by the laity, including women.

67 *John Wesley, whose followers were numerous throughout the Eden Valley.*

John Burgess, in a review of Christianity in Cumbria, wrote, 'Whilst the Dukes of Devonshire and Buccleuch provided Anglican churches for Barrow-in-Furness, miners and poor farmers in Alston were gathering cobbles from the burns for their chapel's walls.' An unusual Methodist minister who was to exert a national appeal was George Bramwell Evens. Born in Hull in 1884, the son of a *gorgio* (non-gypsy) and a *Romanichais* (gypsy woman), he grew up in a religious family. In September 1914, having been rejected by the Armed Forces because of a heart murmur, he was given the care of a small chapel in Carlisle. During the construction of a munitions factory near Gretna, he worked with the labourers, organising a club for them. This led to his being invited to remain in Carlisle, in charge of the principal (but decrepit) Methodist chapel in Fisher Street. A new mission hall was built through his drive and the support, in particular, of Joseph Rank, the wealthy miller and keen supporter of Methodist projects. After moving to different appointments in the West Riding, the minister did not forget the haunts in the Eden Valley where Joseph Fiddler and John Rudd of Carlisle had instructed him in angling, and his good friends included the Potters of Old Parks Farm, near Kirkoswald.

He adopted the name 'Romany' for a series of nature programmes for the BBC North Region, broadcast from Manchester. Under the title *Out with Romany*, they used various sound effects to simulate in a radio studio his country travels with

68 *Rush-bearing at Warcop. Schoolboys in procession bear crosses made of rushes.*

69 *Warcop Rush-bearing. The girls have floral crowns.*

70 *Starry ceiling, Carlisle Cathedral. This fine ceiling was for a time under-drawn.*

dog Raq, horse Comma and *vardo* (four-wheeled caravan). Comma, who drew the van, was so named because he seldom came to a full-stop. Romany's easy manner and love of the countryside were evident in the many books he wrote. When he died, in 1943, his ashes were consigned to Old Parks Farm, arriving at Lazonby in the goods section of a passenger train from Carlisle.

Today Carlisle Cathedral rises in redstone majesty at the heart of the city, presiding over a diocese that takes in the Lake District and reaches to the shores of Morecambe Bay. Despite its stub-end of a nave, the building is impressive. An East Window that is 58 feet high and 32½ feet broad imparts glory, matching in date, style and size the Great West Window of York so closely it is probable that the master mason hailed from the York school of design. To strike all the curves the masons needed to obtain over 260 centres with a compass. Minor pieces of tracery may be taken out for repair without endangering the stability of a window which contains pieces of glass of 14th-century date.

Kenneth Smith, a former librarian of the city, described the building as 'this small gem of a cathedral', mentioning what has a fair claim to be England's most beautiful ceiling, of 'florious blue set with gold stars and coloured bosses'. It was last painted in the early 1970s, and before that in 1856 and 1764. Today's visitors walk under a blue vault and a constellation of 2,816 stars.

Chapter 10

A Romantic Age

What became known as the Romantic Age blossomed between 1760 and 1820, when people with taste, money and leisure responded to a cult known as the Picturesque. Early in the 18th century, Daniel Defoe had found the scenery of the Lake District wild, barren and frightful. He was awestruck by the Pennine escarpment viewed from the Eden Valley. In 1726 Alexander Gordon, an early travel writer, was less interested in landscape than in the Roman history of Cumberland. He portrayed a scene of vanished grandeur that would be described romantically by other writers and artists. Viewing the remnants of what he described as a large Roman *oppidum*, or station, at Netherby, where a garrison once lay, Gordon wrote, 'Here indeed are great marks of a ruinous town, and many inscriptions, pieces of broken sculpture and coins have been found. In the garden I saw a noble statue, at full length, of a man in a sacrificing posture. It is naked, excepting a loose, thin piece of drapery which, coming over his left arm and falling on his right thigh, covers his nudities ... On his head was a *Corona Muralis*, in his left hand a cornucopia, and in his right hand a *Patera*, which he holds over a little altar. His feet, however, were covered by those kinds of *Caligulae* or buskins used by the Romans.' The statue, cut from a single piece of stone, stood in a niche with an estimated length of three feet three inches.

By mid-century, artists, poets and tourists were sharing in the discovery of the Lake Counties portrayed in such accounts and in the paintings, especially of the Lake District, appearing in exhibitions. A peripheral area like the Eden Valley might not have had lakes but there were spectacular sandstone gorges through which the Eden surged, passing here and there places where nature had been tampered with, such as a footpath hewn in a sandstone cliff or a hermit's cell cut from living rock. Wealthy landowners changed or beautified their estates to appeal to those of a Romantic disposition. These were also shooting estates, pheasants being bred from Asian jungle fowl. Rhododendrons, used for game cover, were also in demand. They helped adorn the natural scene.

The Nunnery Walks on the eastern bank of the Eden, where it gushes through a gorge between redstone cliffs, were created during this period. F.S. Williams, writing about the Settle-Carlisle Railway, switched subjects to express appreciation of 'the most beautiful sylvan scenery in Cumberland'. The Walks were of great repute 'on account of their ancient date and their present loveliness'. A hotel occupies the site of a Benedictine nunnery, which at the Dissolution was occupied by a prioress and three nuns. Their revenue from 300 acres and other property was a mere 18 guineas, its small size being attributed to the border conflicts.

Christopher Aglionby, who inherited the estate on the death of his father, laid out the Walks about

71 *Moss-trooper figure in a niche at Netherby Hall, former home of the Graham family.*

1750. Wordsworth, who had family links with Penrith and therefore knew the area well, felt they were unrivalled in beauty. A short Edenside stretch is on a ledge cut into the side of a cliff. Using this man-made path is an exciting experience when the river is in lively mood. Near where the Croglin Beck blends its water with the Eden is a seat. In his *Guide to the Lakes*, the Revd W. Ford referred to the Croglin, pouring along a deep ravine in this last part of its course: 'It first enters this savage dell by a fall of forty feet, forcing its way into a deep cauldron scooped out of the rock, in which the water is agitated and whirled around in boiling eddies till it finds an escape by a narrow opening in one corner, whence it rushes down several leaps, foaming over the large masses that hinder its impetuous progress ...'

72   *William Wordsworth, who considered the Nunnery Walks by the Eden unrivalled in beauty.*

73   *A riverside section of Nunnery Walks (which is on private land).*

F.S. Williams also mentioned Samson's Cave, named after a railway labourer who, during a fight, killed his opponent and fled to the cave. He was discovered, tried and hanged. In Victorian times, the curious might visit the cave using footsteps cut in the rock and, for hand-holds, pieces of iron and wood driven into it at an appropriate height. One visitor who passed 'under overhanging rocks, worn by age, rain, sunshine and storm into such fantastic shapes', felt a sense of relief when he reached a point of safety at the entrance to the underground system. He then disturbed a colony of jackdaws: 'A hawk flew from its eyrie, on a ledge among some stunted shrubs, just where a honeysuckle was coming into flower, strewn with down and feathers.'

Upriver from Nunnery Walks, and on the same bank, are Lacy's Caves. Five rooms had been excavated from particularly soft sandstone in a cliff above the swirling Eden at the behest of Lt Col Samuel Lacy, who lived at Salkeld Hall in the 18th century. Lacy was possibly inspired in his scheme by St Constantine's Caves at Wetheral. It has been suggested that he used the five rooms of the caves

74 *Lacy's Caves, five rooms cut out of particularly soft sandstone by the river.*

as a wine store but the more popular story is that he entertained guests in the novel setting of rooms interconnected by arched doorways and, for a time, employed a resident hermit.

Reference has already been made to the Howards of Corby. The development of their great estate was carried out in a spectacular way on the steep bank of the Eden. Early in the 18th century, Thomas Howard commissioned the landscaping of the riverside: paths led the visitor beside the Eden for about a mile, with a surprise to enjoy every few hundred yards. Water poured from the mouth of a strange beast and followed a stone staircase, the Cascade, into a shady basin pool.

75 *Riverside features carved from the red sandstone beside the River Eden, Corby Castle.*

Beside it was set a statue of Lord Nelson, carved soon after his victory and death at Trafalgar. A massive statue of Polyphemus was known to the locals as 'Belted Will' and a temple was approached via a green track. Ladies' Walk, a mile-long riverside stretch between Langwathby and Edenhall, is so named because it appealed to the Musgrave ladies who were brought by horse-drawn carriage to one end and collected at the other. The old walk having been blocked here and there by landslides, a new path has been laid at a higher level.

In 1850 the eccentric William Mounsey, of Castleton House by the lower reaches of the Eden, walked beside the river from Solway to its source beyond Hell Gill. He chiselled enigmatic inscriptions on the sandstone cliffs of the Eden Gorge and also on a cliff near Armathwaite, where in 1855 he reproduced lines from Isaac Walton, angler:

> Oh the fisher's gentle life
> Happiest is of any;
> Void of pleasur [sic] full of strife
> And beloved by many;
> Others joys are but toys
> And to be lamented
> Only this a pleasure is.

76 *Inscription by William Mounsey of Castlehead on an Edenside cliff near Armathwaite.*

One of the rounded faces is adorned by a cap that resembles the old-style bee skep. Mounsey commemorated his journey by raising at the source of the Eden a memorial stone, inscribed in Latin and Greek, which recorded that this lone traveller 'fulfilled his view to the Genius and nymphs of the Eden' on 15 March. Because local people could not understand the inscription, and Mounsey's dark beard led them to mistake him for a Jew, the memorial became known as 'the Jew Stone'. Navvies taking time off from construction work on the Settle-Carlisle railway broke it up but, years later, the pieces were collected and kept in a garage at Kirkby Stephen, then used for reference in order to create a representation of the Jew Stone on the Green at Outhgill, Mallerstang.

The language of the Age of Romance endures in tourist literature, arousing the curiosity of visitors and offsetting the grim realities of modern life. In a leaflet entitled *Alston Moor, 'Heart of the Northern Pennines'*, great fells stand 'at the head of England's mountain backbone' and the rivers Tyne, Wear and Tees 'spring forth as infants among the hills'. The landscape transcends human scale, yet 'man has etched his history of endeavour laboriously over these hillsides'. A secret preserved by geographical remoteness is now 'easily accessible to discerning travellers bent on discovering somewhere new; somewhere that is entirely different'.

Chapter 11

Lead Mining

Hutchinson, writing at the close of the 18th century, described the small market town of Alston as lying in a narrow valley 'over which mountains frown with a melancholy sterility and nakedness'. Alston, he added, was 'at the declivity of a steep hill, inhabited by miners'. Not in Derbyshire or even Cornwall was there so peculiarly wild a spot as Alston Moor, where 'all that the earth produces is from its bowels' and 'where the people also are so generally subterraneous'.

Alston became a boom town in the early 19th century when lead, silver, copper, iron and zinc were being mined. The mineral veins had formed when the near vertical geological faults filled with solutions which then cooled. Silver mined at Alston and Caldbeck was being minted at Carlisle in the 13th century. The best of the lead seams ran north-east to south-west and were split diagonally by what 'T'Owd Man', a term for past generations of miners, knew as the Great Sulphur Seam, evident on the north and north-east slopes of Cross Fell.

77   Nenthead miners.

North Pennine roads are like switchbacks. The turnpike linking Alston with Penrith was made on the instructions of the Commissioners of Greenwich Hospital, who had become considerable landowners. They advanced £30,344 for the track through South Tyne and appointed McAdam as their engineer. A post coach was inaugurated between Hexham and Penrith on 26 September 1828, which went via Hartside Cross, but in the following year a coach hauled by four horses was traversing the route.

The road from Alston to Teesdale is a highway in a literal sense, making an unremitting climb to Yad Moss, 1,960 feet above sea level. The topographer Leland, writing of what he called 'Yade More', credited it with being the source of the Tees, whereas it was but a tributary of the great river that 'takith a course among rokkes and reyving divers other small hopes or bekkes'. Traces of mining on Alston Moor are everywhere evident but accurate dating is uncertain, the evidence of early workings having been removed by later projects. In the late 19th century, when Chester Armstrong, son of a lead miner, penned *Pilgrimage from Nenthead*, life was bleak and austere. The people about whom he wrote were dour and serious-minded, their lives bounded by the nearest horizons and by strict rules of work and play. Today, the newly restored mine complex at Nenthead plus the other ruined buildings, with cracked or broken slates, testify to the presence of a once great industry. Spoil heaps are bare, except where they are cushioned by spring sandwort, a lead-tolerant plant with star-like white flowers. Deserted adits and shafts are too dangerous to explore. Richard Watson, a 'Teesdale Bard', wrote:

> Large rubbish heaps along the hillside show
> The vast extent of hollow ground below.

78 *Lead miners at Nenthead.*

It is believed that the Romans mined lead on the East Fellside, exploiting veins in deep glacial valleys such as Great Rundale above Dufton and Scorton above Hilton. During the reign of Henry II, in the 12th century, mines were being let at an average rent of £100. In 1289 tempers flared between Goan and Henry de Whitby and the miners of Alduneston (Alston) over the excessive felling of timber to be used as props and fuel at the Tynehead mines. A scarcity of the wood needed to smelt ore caused a fall in value, and the squabble led in 1478 to the gold, silver, copper and lead mines in Northumberland, Cumberland and Westmorland being granted for a ten-year spell to four Germans from Cologne and an Englishman. One-fifteenth of the profits was to go to the Crown. German know-how came to the rescue again in 1538, when closed mines were reinvigorated.

On the East Fellside, the mid-17th century saw the Scordale Mines near Hilton being worked by John Bland and Company, and mines at Dufton by one Winder, lord of the manor. A horse pawing the ground on Cross Fell displaced loose turf and topsoil, bringing a profitable seam into view. But the commercial success of lead and silver mining in the North Pennines is related mainly to the ministrations, during a hundred and forty years, of the London Lead Company, a company of mainly Quaker shareholders which was concerned with mining in the north of England and in Derbyshire, Wales and Ireland from 1692 to 1905.

The company's involvement with the North Pennine orefield was a sequel to the beheading for treason of James Radcliffe, 3rd Earl of Derwentwater, who owned the Manor of Alston Moor. James had played a part in the first Jacobite Rebellion of 1715. His estate, forfeited to the Crown, was in 1735 granted to the Royal Hospital for Seamen at Greenwich. Most of the local mining leases were let by the Greenwich Hospital to Colonel George Liddell, who in 1745 constructed a smelt mill. When the Liddell leases were transferred to the London Lead Company it became the major employer in the area, an enlightened attitude towards mining bringing into existence a network of durable service roads to replace the old *gal* (horse) tracks and badly maintained turnpike roads.

Hartside, zig-zagging up the Pennine escarpment and clearing it at an elevation of over 1,900 feet above sea level, was one such road. Another, connecting Knock with Garrigill by way of Knockergill pass, levelled out at an impressive 2,478 feet. Wheeled traffic for lead and stores made the plodding *gals* redundant. The strings of 25 pack animals, a bell attached to the leader giving notice of their approach, became confined to memory. They had been muzzled to prevent their dining on vegetation poisoned by lead. The London Lead Company arranged for the former annual payment to miners to be succeeded by a monthly subsistence one, as outlined by Thomas Dodd who was chief mine agent from 1785 until 1816.

Silverband, under Great Dun Fell, had an especially remote situation. With an elevation of about 2,300 feet, it was the highest mine in Britain. The approach was by a long, steep route from the hamlet of Knock. A mining map shows mine workings as they were in 1846, under the London Lead Company. But not all the mines were at a high level. At Hartley, near Kirkby Stephen, in about 1750, Sir Philip Musgrave constructed a smelt mill, having a handy reserve of coal on Hartley Fell. He leased out most of his mines on the understanding that his mill would deal with their smelting. Originally bell-pits were in use, but by 1884 the lead and copper were almost exhausted. The last flourish of activity, both here and at Silverband, was to recover barytes, used in preparing 'mud' for drilling purposes.

Lead, in the form of natural compound lead sulphide, known as *galena*, accounted for a small proportion of a mineral vein, which was also filled by 'gangue', or other minerals, notably fluorspar and barytes. The highest proportion of lead to 'gangue' occurred in the 'flats'. Miners worked in pairs up to the closure of the 19th century, the rock being broken up by the hand-drilling of holes into which gunpowder was placed. It was definitely a two-man job, one miner holding a 'jumper' (chisel),

79 *A lead-mining adit with worn sleepers to which rails were once connected.*

80 *A preserved lead-mining tub.*

the other striking it with a hammer. A more ancient process was known as 'stope and feathers': a hole bored with the help of a 'jumper' was packed with iron 'feathers', each about eight inches long. The 'stope', a tapering iron wedge, was hammered in between them, shattering the rock.

Generations of miners, known collectively as t'Owd Man, worked in a constricted underworld, access to which was down shafts and along adits. Before horse-levels became common, mined ore was transported on barrows or sleds. Winches or gins were available to hoist ore up the shafts. After horse-levels became available, rails were laid so that laden tubs of ore might be hauled by animals. Arches and vaults were skilfully fashioned of dry stone, some arches supporting the enormous weight of 'deads', waste material left underground. There was a time when illumination was provided by candles made in Kirkby Stephen. These were attached to mine walls with knobs of clay. When not in use, they were kept in tin boxes so the rats would not devour them.

It was an unhealthy environment. Confined in tight and dusty passages, many miners succumbed to 'gruver's sickness', a form of silicosis, and died while in their thirties. Yet a lead miner's favourite topic was mining. When a shift was over on a winter day, several mates would gather in a cottage or even in a public house to discuss mining topics. Black twist was stuffed into the bowls of clay pipes and kindled by being held between the bars of the fire grate. Broken clay pipes have been found throughout the North Pennine orefield.

Mined ore was placed in a 'bouse team', or walled compartment. Samples were tested and monitored by the Assayer, who worked in an elegant Assay House of the type seen at Nenthead, nowadays a prime site for the study of the lead-mining industry. The Assay House, dating from 1833 and rebuilt in 1855, has its distinctive appearance created by some especially large windows which maximise the spread of natural light. Bouse, a mixture of rock, spar and *galena*, was picked over by hand then crushed using a 'buckler', or hammer. Separation of the *galena* from other material took place in a flow of water, the *galena* being the densest substance and settling first. Washer boys were employed and a mining song credited to Thomas Raine and dating from the 1860s began:

It's early in the morning,
We rise at five o'clock,
And the little lads come to the door
To knock, knock, knock.
So come, my little washer boys,
Come, let's away,
We're bound down to slavery
For fourpence a day.

81 *Stylish architecture. The upper part of a restored Assay House at Nenthead.*

At Nenthead, the smelt mill chimney was set high on the fell so that the poisonous fumes would not affect the villagers or, indeed, pollute the best land. Small boys were set to work cleaning out the long flue and recovering any lead or silver that had condensed on its sides. The smelters were most handsomely remunerated. They roasted, then smelted, the ore until molten lead might be poured into moulds to form pigs, or ingots, and they had a hard life, a shift extending over 12 hours. Almost every smelting mill had a different mode of working, but water power was employed, one waterwheel at Nenthead having a diameter of 50 feet. A pair of wheels, each with a diameter of 45 feet, was used at the Haggs dressing plant. Made in Scotland in the late 18th century, they were erected at Nentsberry by Ralph Atkinson and needed little maintenance.

Lead ore production on Alston Moor reached its peak in the decade from 1817 to 1827 when over a thousand miners produced 217,000 'bings' (each of 8 cwt), valued at over £1 million. The major engineering achievement was the Nent Force Level. Running underground from Nenthead to Alston, a distance of four and a half miles, it drained the mines in the Nent Valley and allowed for deeper working. This was another project in which the celebrated engineer Smeaton was involved and the cost was a swingeing £81,000. The level also acted for a while as an underground canal, along which 30ft barges carried 'bouse'. Tourists revelled in the candlelit voyage from Alston to an underground waterfall.

Arthur Raistrick, Quaker historian, wrote of the company influence on farming: 'This policy, which in some form or other spread to all the mining areas, created the very extensive belt of intake that is now an essential part of the mining landscape.' Lead mining augmented a type of farming that was mainly pastoral, on the Norse pattern, with flocks of hill sheep and cattle thriving on coarse vegetation. Some beasts were sold off, others kept as breeding stock, and yet

82   *Arthur Raistrick, who chronicled the history of Quaker activity in the North Pennine orefield.*

more slaughtered and then cured for winter consumption. The enclosure movement did not affect local landowning until the 1820s. William Wallace, a mining engineer for the London Lead Company, recorded that 'during the last century, and up to the year 1840, bread was made of rye meal; very little wheat was used, but a considerable quantity of oat meal. The meals and bread stuffs were chiefly brought from the valley of the Eden over the rough mountain passes on the backs of ponies.' Nenthead became famous for its potatoes and a Leek Club was formed.

The unsung heroes were miners working in a remote area such as Cashwell, on Cross Fell. The mining company supplied buildings, beds, cooking facilities, fuel and running water, and the men had a five-day week, subsisting on their own food and sleeping in their own bedding. The weekend was spent in the comparative luxury of home. On the long walk to the mine a man carried his possessions in a 'wallet', which resembled a long pillow case with an opening at the centre. Spare clothes and food were stacked in such a way that the 'wallet' could be carried over a shoulder, the weight on either side being in balance. In winter they walked in darkness, judging whether they were on the right track by the direction of the wind, which they had noted on leaving home. Their clogs were ideal for turning 'snow broth' but attracted hard snow, a great lump forming on the soles unless pieces of leather were nailed to them.

Lodging 'shops' were grim, as noted by a report into child employment of 1842. The lodging-rooms inspected were 'not fit for swine to live in. In one house there were 16 bedsteads in the room upstairs and 50 occupied these beds at the same time. We could not always get all in together but we got in when we could.' Three sleepers might lie side by side, with a fourth at the foot of the bed. A man had several times to get out of bed and sit up in the night, 'to make room for my little brothers, who were there as washers [separating *galena* from dross]. After I had been there two years, rules were laid down, and two men were appointed by the master to clean the house upstairs twice a week. The lower apartment had to be cleaned twice a day. Then the shop floor was boarded and

83   *Nenthead folk in gala mood.*

84   *Sunday School treat at Nenthead. Horses and carts transport scholars to the train at Alston for a day at Whitley Bay.*

two tables were place in the shop. After that two more shops were fitted up, but the increase of workmen more then kept up with the increased accommodation. The breathing at night when all were in bed was dreadful.'

By and large, the miners were grave, reflective men who did not fritter away their earnings on ale and rarely used bad language. Many were devout Methodists. John Wesley preached at Nenthead in 1748 and 1770, so most of the Methodists were Wesleyans. The Primitive Methodists, known as 'Prims', were also in evidence. In the 19th century a Mr Forster wrote, 'The lead miners are remarkably intelligent and well-educated. There are books in every cottage. Attendance at public worship is the rule, not the exception, and profane language is scarcely ever heard.'

The Quakers supplied the workforce with a free medical service. Workmen injured or ruined in health received assistance from a company fund. Mining families had a reliable income, a miner being paid an agreed rate per 'bing' of ore produced or per fathom of ground cut, the wage often related to the current price of lead. The London Lead Company not only guaranteed a minimum wage sufficient to cover food and clothing, irrespective of lead prices, but enabled a miner and his family to have a cottage and several acres of land on the edge of the moor for a cow-house and pigsty and, in some cases, rights to pasture sheep on the moor.

The London Lead Company was wound down in 1882, unable to compete with the lower cost of imported lead, which became significant after 1870. Other companies took over the local lead and silver production, but by this time most of the North Pennine mineral veins had been virtually picked clean. The company was officially wound up in 1905. Mining at Nenthead, which at its peak in 1841 had employed 3,000 men, ended in 1919. When the last level closed just fifty men were employed in the industry. The labour force in the previous year, before the closure of other levels, had been two hundred. Miners and their families had sustained two chapels and a reading-room.

In his *Directory* of 1901, Bulmer noted that Nenthead Ecclesiastical District was rich in mineral wealth and added, 'The hill, which rises

85 *William Shaw of Keswick, an authority on mining in the Lake Counties.*

above the village, is so honeycombed and tunnelled with subterraneous workings that, it is said, a person may enter at Nenthead and, after wandering about for seven or eight miles, may emerge on the Durham side of the Hill.' Elsewhere, 'healthy moorlands form its distinguishing feature, and over a wide extent the traveller searches in vain for a single spot of beauty on which to feast his weary eyes … Small trout abound in the rivers, and grouse upon the moors, where grow clustered bramble-like cranberries, commonly called cloud-berries.' Many miners found alternative employment at Haltwhistle and in Weardale. Those who had farmed part-time now devoted the whole of their attention to agriculture. Heaps of discarded material were picked over for fluorspar, which was needed as a flux by the steel industry. Lead mining had undoubtedly stimulated progress in what had been remote little villages: Garrigill had a piped water supply in 1904, a sewerage scheme in 1926 and electricity in 1936.

86   *Eric Richardson of Nenthead, one of the latter-day leadminers.*

Eric Richardson, the source of most of my information about Nenthead, lost his father Joseph in a roof-fall that occurred in 1916. Joseph was 42 years of age. Mother was left to bring up six girls and three boys in a modest house at Overwater. She had to go out to work and turned to some advantage her skill at bread-making. The bread was supplied to Italian workers employed by the Vielle Montagne Zinc Co., of Belgium, successors of the Nenthead and Tynedale Lead and Zinc Company, who had increased silver production and continued the smelting process until the mill closed in 1896. Barium compounds, which had been a useless by-product of the lead-mining industry, now found industrial applications in pigment manufacture, as mordants in textile dyeing, in the case-hardening of steel and in the manufacture of glass and enamel. They imparted body to cloth, paper, rubber, linoleum and lithographic inks and were even used to produce blemish-free bricks. Spoil heaps were rifled for a once-despised by-product.

Lead mining in the North Pennines inspired Wystan Hugh Auden, one of the finest poets of the 20th century. When Alan Myers and Robert Forsythe compiled

87 *The big waterwheel at Killhope, upper Weardale, a mining complex just over the hill from Nenthead.*

a booklet about the connection, in 1999, Auden was dubbed 'Pennine Poet'. A doctor's son, he was born in York in 1907 but grew up in Birmingham, and was so moved by the industrial landscape that while at Oxford he regularly walked beside the gasworks. His fascination with lead mining dated from family holidays in Wales and Derbyshire just before and during the First World War. He visited the North Pennines in 1919 and five years later was writing poems about Alston Moor and Allendale. He described his impressions of the pumping station at Cashwell Mine, on the slopes of Cross Fell. Stimulated by his 'beloved chilly North', as Christopher Isherwood wrote, Auden was fond of cold conditions. In an article he wrote for *Home and Garden*, he called the north the Never-Never Land of his dreams.

The heyday of lead mining, when the population of the North Pennines rose to around 25,000, is vividly recalled at Nenthead and Killhope, the last-named at Wearhead just over the fell, where a huge waterwheel turns. Restoration work has tidied up the sites and saved mine buildings, and opened up horse-levels to give visitors an idea of life underground. At Nenthead, one of the earliest purpose-built industrial villages in Britain, situated at 1,100 feet, a spectacular exhibit illustrates the use of various types of waterwheel. Visitors may operate the controls themselves. This is supplemented with information about the past and Nenthead Mines is now a scheduled Ancient Monument with areas designated as Sites of Special Scientific Interest (SSSI).

Chapter 12

Road and Rail

The Old Highway from Wensleydale via Cotter End provided a steep and rutted entry into the Eden Valley. William Camden in *Britannia* (1590) described the landscape as being 'waste, solitary, unpleasant and unsightly, so mute and so still'. He erroneously gave Eden's source as 'Hugh Morvill's hill', since known as Hugh's Seat (2,257 feet), an allusion to Sir Hugh de Morville who, during the reign of Henry II, owned Pendragon Castle in Mallerstang. He and three other knights were implicated in the murder of Thomas a Becket in Canterbury Cathedral.

Lady Anne Clifford used the Old Highway en route for Pendragon on 8 October 1663. She travelled by horse-drawn coach, 'where I think Coach never went before', finding the way steep and stony. Crossing Hellgill Bridge, she entered Westmorland. An historic route across Stainmore, from Bowes to Brough, was probably used by Bronze-Age folk and, most certainly, by the Romans. The habitable parts of Stainmore lie at around 900 feet but the road clears the 1,000ft contour.

88 *Mitred head of Thomas à Becket in stained glass at Horton-in-Ribblesdale. Hugh de Morville, one of the knights implicated in Becket's murder, had a considerable tract of land at the head of the Eden Valley. His name is commemorated in Hugh's Seat, a fell near the source of the Eden.*

Each autumn, from the 17th century to the railway age of the 19th, droves of Scottish cattle were seen on north-south roads and tracks. The cattle were small, vulgar (black) animals known as 'kyloes' that would thrive anywhere, having been reared on impoverished ground in the Highlands and Islands. Along with beasts from Wales and Ireland, the stock met the demand for fresh beef generated by the rapid growth of industrialising towns. A popular droving route for Scottish cattle, as noted by Kenneth K. Bonsor in *The Drovers* (1970), was past Bewcastle and then southwards through the Eden Valley to Melmerby, Ousby, Kirkland, Newbiggin, Long Marton and Appleby. Journey's end was the great fair at Brough Hill, where around 10,000 Scottish cattle, as well as Cumbrian stock, might have been assembled for sale.

H.F. Oliphant, writing in *Cumbria* (1972), noted that the type of cattle associated with Dumfries had the local name of Galloway. Each October, the Sands Market at Dumfries was full of black cattle for Carlisle, Brough Hill, Norfolk and a scattering of other places in the Midlands and South. Thomas Dundas, a Carlisle cattle dealer, was fined at Dumfries in August 1812 for driving cattle on the Sabbath. St Faith's Fair, near Norwich, was renowned for the sale of such cattle. Driving the beasts from Scotland to Norfolk cost a drover from 18s. to 20s. a head, but Norfolk was attractive as it had excellent grazing on rich flat land where progressive farmers were growing clover, sanfoin and vast acreages of turnips.

The Scottish and North Country cattle were intended to be sold at Smithfield Market in London. By using upland tracks from the border, the drovers and their stock might maintain a leisurely pace of 10 to 12 miles a day. Before the enclosures, the stock had free grazing wherever they rested for the night. Oatmeal made into porridge was a favourite food. The basis of 'haverbread', oatmeal was carried in a 'haversack' (a name still used by present-day ramblers). In 1663, the year Lady Anne braved the rigours of the Old Highway, 18,574 head of cattle passed through Carlisle. A toll of eight pence per head was exacted.

Local researchers in Kirkby Stephen library discovered another reason why drovers chose high ground with broad vistas: there was the threat of ambush. At the Quarter Sessions in Northallerton on 2 August 1692, two 'persons' were accused of robbing a drover from Kaber in Westmorland of £144 7s. 'at or near Ellerbecke in the hundred of Gilling West'. The court recommended that those who lived in the said hundred should repay the drover the said sum 'without any further trouble'. Another droving risk was cattle disease, a general term for which – 'the murrain' – covered a multitude of complaints, including foot and mouth disease, tuberculosis, sheep pox or scab.

J.D. Marshall has recorded that animals leaving Carlisle, where many thousands were recorded each year by the toll-takers, might go down the old Penrith coach road to High Hesket (Broadfield) and then via Penrith into the Eden Valley.

89 *Jagger ponies, forming a packhorse train. Drawn by W. Gilbert Foster for a book by Edmund Bogg.*

A great many more would follow the foothills of Eden via Hilton and Dufton to Brough. Daniel Scott (1899) mentioned the occasional herds passing along the ancient track over Cotter End and Hell Gill – the Old Highway, in fact. Scottish cattle were offered for sale at Hawes and on the Great Close, Malham Moor. When the animals showed signs of fatigue, 'it was no uncommon thing to see one of the men who carried a bagpipe play some lively air as he marched in front of the drove.'

Until the transport revolution in the early part of the 19th century, packhorses carried goods from place to place. Daniel Scott, writing about bygone Westmorland, alluded to a procession of men and horses with miscellaneous goods that made their way out of the Yorkshire Dales to Kirkby Stephen and the north. The drivers from Garsdale and Grisedale came over the moor from Shaw Paddock to Aisgill and the old Thrang Bridge in Mallerstang. Here they were met by strings of packhorses and men coming from the east country by Hell Gill. 'The thrifty wives and daughters of the dales used to go up to Hell Gill Bridge and spread out stalls and baskets, stored with cakes, nuts, apples and bottles of home-made herb beer.'

Road transport in the mid-18th century was restricted to a few carts and wagons. *Jollies Directory of Cumberland* said of Carlisle at this time, 'Provisions rose in price, butchers began to sell their meat by weight, the street manure was sold, and the country wore a more cultivated aspect.' By the first decade of the 19th century, the city had increased in population, wealth and refinement, mainly through the introduction of cotton manufacture in its various branches, and Jollies mentioned five banks, two of which issued notes on their own account.

90   *Horse and cart days. The Market Place at Carlisle.*

91   *Market Place, Carlisle complete with motor vehicles.*

Into Carlisle, by road or the river, came iron, tar, slates, staves, salt, sugar and rum. From the city went grain, potatoes, oak bark, oatmeal, flour, timber, lead, freestone, herrings, alabaster and barrel staves.

Access to the North Pennines is provided by the A686 from Penrith to Alston. At Hartside the road zig-zags to an elevation of almost 2,000 feet and traffic is occasionally buffeted by the Helm Wind, its roaring probably engendering the local belief in witches and warlocks. Over a century ago, stallholders attending the market at Alston from 'the other side of the fell', from Langwathby, Melmerby, Gamblesby and Renwick, used this route, the procession of carts beginning at around 5 a.m. Time was allowed to rest the horses, but it was not unknown for the wind to overturn a cart. On them was produce grown on the fertile red acres of Edenvale, including apples and pears from walled orchards and blackberries gathered from hedgerows.

Martha James, a daughter of the Revd Octavius James of Clarghyll Hall, Alston, who wrote over thirty books, used the drama of man's struggle against the elements to vivid effect. She took a hero, Davie Armstrong, over Hartside on horseback when all the fiends of Cross Fell howled and whirled the snow into great drifts. Elizabeth Birkett, a contributor to the magazine *Cumbria*, recorded the local tradition that witches from the area departed when the first motor cars appeared on Hartside and the reek of petrol was in the air. 'They may fly back in a night of storm when snow blocks the road west, but surely on moonlit nights the shades of Betty Greenhow, Harry Chicken, Sally Toppin and Michael Harker ride down in ghostly carts to hold concourse in Alston market place and buy and sell with their shadowy long-gone customers.'

A track across the Pennines between Slaggyford near Alston and Croglin was once well used by shepherds with stock to be sold in the market at Lazonby. Women from Knaresdale crossed when seeking recalcitrant husbands at the *Robin Hood* in Croglin. Elizabeth Birkett, who contributed many pieces about Alston to *Cumbria*, sent us verses from a ditty about the 'Croglin Watties', men and women who missed the mountain track and spent a bitter winter night on the moors. At daybreak they plodded down to the *Malt Shovel* in Slaggyford and later in the afternoon reached Hanging Shaw Farm, where they had been invited to dance and make merry.

The dawning of the railway age, which offered rapid and dependable transport, led to great social changes. Today the West Coast mainline trains stop at Penrith and the Settle-Carlisle has four stations in the Eden Valley. The North Eastern Railway from Newcastle initially terminated at a red brick structure in London Road, Carlisle. The stonework for the viaduct spanning the Eden at Wetheral, a structure 625 feet long with five massive arches and piers attaining a maximum height of a hundred feet, was quarried at Newbiggin, and the infill material came from local sources. Henry Howard of Corby Castle laid the first stone in March 1830. There were branch lines to Alston and Allendale.

The first ticket at Wetheral was issued in 1837, when the cost of a return journey to Carlisle was one shilling. The passenger who received the ticket was instructed to show it to the station master at Carlisle before taking his seat for the return journey. Amongst the small print was a notice that 'no gratuity is allowed to be taken by any guard, porter or other servant of the company.' The sandstone viaduct at Wetheral caught the attention of William Wordsworth, who wrote, 'the banks of the river Eden and Corby are well worthy of notice on account of their natural beauty and the viaducts which have recently been carried over the bed of the river and over a neighbouring ravine.' Access to the riverbank was by way of 91 steps formed of old stone sleepers.

The first stone of Citadel Station, Carlisle was laid amidst great privacy in March 1847. Once it was opened to the public, a writer in the *Carlisle Patriot* observed that the ceremony had signalled the end of small market town life in Carlisle and the beginning of an era that would surely see industry boom: 'The railways are a quick way to link the agricultural districts of the North with the Metropolis.' Initiated jointly by the Lancaster and Carlisle Railway, in the south, and the Caledonian Railway Company, the station was built of Yorkshire stone

92 *The Citadel, Carlisle with attendant cars.*

and spread itself over nine acres, having eight platforms, three 'throughs' and five bays. The 'through' platforms, each about 1,000 yards long, might be used for either north- or south-bound traffic.

The architect Sir William Tite chose Victorian Tudor for his design. A lengthy, irregular, two-storeyed frontage was adorned by a clock tower-cum-octagonal lantern, and the crests of the two companies flanked the main entrance. By including mullioned windows and prominent chimneys, the architect went a good way to matching the new station building with the nearby Citadel law courts and what remained of the city walls. In the main waiting room were neo-Tudor fireplaces with Latin inscriptions translatable as 'God has made us these places of rest.' The Lancaster and Carlisle became part of the Lancaster and North Western Railway Company which, together with the Caledonian, introduced an Anglo-Scottish service. Carlisle's strategic position eventually attracted seven private companies, each of which was represented on a joint committee. The committee's head, known as the station superintendent, wore top hat and morning coat. The Midland, operating from London St Pancras via Derby and Leeds, traversed the Eden Valley.

Carlisle was initially an 'open' station, the public having the right of way from Court Square across the station to the viaduct entrance. Passengers had their tickets collected in advance of arrival. On non-corridor trains, tickets were collected at the station before Carlisle: from the east this was at Scotby; from the south at Wreay, and from the north at Rockcliffe. Trains from Silloth were permitted to run into No. 8 bay, a barrier being set up which didn't contravene the open station plan. After years of legal argument, the LMS eventually took over the station which became 'closed'.

When, in 1932, James S. Leslie became district inspector on the Carlisle to Beattock Summit section, the station was administered from Glasgow, but the Carlisle staff, jealous of the old joint committee management, treated outsiders with suspicion. During the Second World War the occupants of troop trains passing from Scotland to England and vice versa were fed at Carlisle. When the 'Queens', ocean liners taken over for the transport of troops, docked on the Clyde, a record number of 148 troop trains were dealt with in one day.

The Port Carlisle Dock & Railway Company, promoted in 1852 and opened on 4 August 1853, followed the course of the waterway built by the Carlisle Canal Company, a waterway authorised by an Act of Parliament of 6 April 1819. The canal, 11 miles long and opened on 12 March 1823, linked Carlisle and Fisher's Cross (renamed Port Carlisle) with the sea. This was shorter and safer than navigating along the River Eden and the Solway Firth. The tidal dock facilities of Port Carlisle comprised little more than a wooden jetty extending beyond the shore. When completed, the canal permitted vessels of 100 tons to reach the basin at Carlisle. A passenger service was operated using a long open boat.

93 *Citadel Station, Carlisle. Originally, seven companies were involved in its operation.*

The Carlisle & Liverpool Steam Navigation Company, which was associated with Port Carlisle, lived up to its name. The first ship, in 1825, was called *Solway*, and the second ship bore the name *Cumberland*, and for a quarter of a century these two vessels operated a weekly service between Carlisle and Liverpool. A passenger leaving Carlisle in the morning arrived at Liverpool in the afternoon. Paddle steamers were brought into service when the Carlisle and Annan Steam Navigation Company provided competition using this type of craft but, with much railway competition, Port Carlisle ceased to prosper and the waterway was abandoned in 1853. The railway was extended to Silloth, where a harbour took sea traffic, but when Mr Beeching lopped off thousands of miles of track the city of Carlisle lost its Silloth and Waverley lines.

Carlisle continues to be one of the main stations in the land. The electrified main line sweeps round the curve of the station. Kingmoor Yard is used to switch freight to Scottish locomotives and to receive from the Clyde coal en route to power stations in South Yorkshire and North Nottinghamshire. On the other hand, the Eden Valley line, intended to operate from Warcop to Brough before crossing Stainmore, foundered when local farmers refused to sell land. The line was promptly re-routed via Musgrave and Kirkby Stephen.

For a century the North Eastern operated a line sixty miles long which linked Darlington with Tebay and Penrith. A single line between Barnard Castle and Tebay had been opened by the South Durham & Lancashire Union Railway in 1861, which was absorbed by the Stockton & Darlington Railway in 1863 and, later that year, by the North Eastern Railway. The adventurous line crossed Stainmore at an elevation of 1,370 feet and connected the coalfields of South

Durham with the blast furnaces of Barrow and West Cumberland. Railway enthusiasts mourn the loss of the line, and especially Belah, a metal viaduct of 16 spans, 1,040 feet long and 196 feet high. Each of the piers had six columns a foot in diameter set in parallel rows of three and strengthened by cross-bracing every five feet. This marvel of Victorian enterprise was built in 43 days, the engineer being Thomas Bouch, who was born in Thursby, near Carlisle, in 1822.

The railway split at Kirkby Stephen, one line going to Penrith via Appleby and the other to Tebay and the London and North Western line, thence along the Furness coast to Barrow. Peak time for freight was in the 1880s when the line carried a million tons of coke annually. The Barrow iron and steel works eventually sourcing fuel from elsewhere caused the line to be closed in 1962. The last length in use served Hartley Quarry until 1975. A once-busy stretch of railway between Kirkby Stephen and Newbiggin-on-Lune is now a footpath, popular with industrial archaeologists and naturalists. In springtime the disturbed but well-drained area favours an abundance of orchids.

With the Settle-Carlisle railway, last of the great Victorian transport ventures, the Midland Company acquired a busy middle route to Scotland. Frustrated at an arrangement which gave them limited use of the Lancaster-Carlisle, reached via the branch line from Ingleton in which the two companies had shares, they determined to run their trains to the border city on their own tracks. A scheme proposed by local landowners to operate a railway from Settle to Hawes was modified to provide a direct route to Carlisle with a branch to Hawes. Built in the 1870s with a modicum of machinery and 6,000 workers, the Settle-Carlisle scheme made good use of two north-south valleys, Eden and Ribble.

94 *Birkett Cutting, as portrayed in F.S. Williams' history of the railway.*

95   *Goods train in a siding at Aisgill, highest point on the Settle-Carlisle system. The signal box is preserved in Derbyshire.*

Of the five contracts, No. 2, extending from Dent Head to Kirkby Stephen, passed through a stock-rearing district with only one arable field in view. The construction work began in September 1869 and in the following year Parkin Blades, an agent for Sir Richard Tufton, lord of the manor of Mallerstang, cut the first sod of the Westmorland section. Joseph Firbank secured Contract No. 3, lying between a point north of Smardale viaduct near Kirkby Stephen and another south of Crowdundle beck, a distance of 14½ miles. Firbank chose Appleby for his headquarters. Key members of his contracting firm met each Boxing Day, in whatever part of the world they might have been engaged, for dinner and entertainment. In 1871 they assembled at the *Crown and Cushion* hotel at Appleby. The health of Joseph Firbank and his manager, Mr J. Throstle, was toasted, and violin, concertina and banjo made an 'agreeable and pleasant concert'. At the peak of activity, Firbank mustered four locomotives, 17 portable engines and steam cranes, over 100 horses, and 500 earth wagons that moved on 2,000 tons of temporary rails. In 1873 the workforce numbered 1,400.

Those employed in the remoter areas were accommodated in cottages and 130 contractors' huts. The 'hut villages' of Contract No. 3 included Battle Barrow Bank, near Long Marton, and the Helm, where a 600-yard tunnel was being driven through solid rock, limestone and grit. The tunnel was lined with bricks produced at a works on site. Children of the workers were provided with a school and Miss Clarke, daughter of the Revd Thomas Clarke, vicar of Ormside, was appointed teacher, her father, as Scripture Reader, spending much of his time visiting the railway workers, 'both on the line and in other huts'.

Three navvies living at the Helm were brought before the Appleby magistrates in 1874 and fined after being found guilty of stealing 'wooden fixtures' from a hut belonging to Mr Firbank, the value of the stolen items being one sovereign. Dry navvy throats were lubricated with much ale and it was reported in the local press that at Appleby in 1873, 'Considering it is a small rural town of a few streets it is something remarkable that it should require nearly 20 public houses and breweries to minister to the [imbibing] propensities of its inhabitants.' The sale of ale at unlicensed huts was initially the concern of Mr Thomas Swindells, supervisor of excise, and in June 1874 James Whitehead,

96   *The now disused viaduct in Smardale, a link on the old rail route between Kirkby Stephen and Tebay.*

'an elderly man', was fined heavily for this offence. In October 1872 a navvy named Charles Fox was in custody at Kirkby Stephen, charged with the theft of a valuable terrier. The police traced the prisoner to Dent Head, where he claimed the dog had followed him. He had sold it to raise money for beer.

The Settle-Carlisle line, designed as an all-weather route, needed an impressive number of viaducts and tunnels. Fitted with new steel tracks and up-to-the-minute signalling equipment, it was opened to goods traffic in August 1875. The first passenger train traversed the line on 1 May of the following year. Visitors to the Eden Valley were astonished at the scale of engineering. The most imposing viaduct in the Eden Valley, spanning the Scandal Beck, absorbed some 60,000 tons of limestone and attained a maximum height of 130 feet. The original design, for a second set of six arches at a lower level, between two heavy piers, was scrapped. But the faith of the engineers in lofty piers was justified. This was a giant in seclusion, remote from villages and good roads, reached along narrow hedge-bordered lanes. Most of the Eden Valley stations had rural settings and names that fascinated early travellers: Long Marton, Newbiggin, Culgaith, Langwathby, Little Salkeld, Lazonby, Armathwaite. In the 1900s, trippers from Yorkshire and Lancashire industrial towns arrived at Langwathby by rail and were met at the station by horse-drawn carriages that conveyed them through Penrith to Ullswater. Tom Glaister photographed them at Langwathby and had copies of the photographs to sell to the trippers when they returned to the station.

In the glory days of steam, the stationmaster, complete with 'scrambled egg' on the neb of his smart cap, had a varied staff. Jack Hodgson, a native of Langwathby

97 (left) *Charles Stanley Sharland, a Tasmanian engineer who surveyed the route to be taken by the Settle-Carlisle railway.*

98 (middle) *John Crossley, the Midland Railway's chief engineer, supervised the construction of the Settle-Carlisle line.*

99 (right) *James Allport, general manager of the Midland when the Settle-Carlisle project was mooted.*

who began work for the Midland Railway in 1897, related how the horses owned by the contractor were taken to the River Eden to have their legs washed but a flash flood drowned three of the men. The company stabled three horses at Langwathby station and was able to convey drays full of parcels to Penrith, five miles away. Two journeys were made each day until 1908, when an alternative route was inaugurated.

The higher reaches of the Settle-Carlisle railway were exposed to severe winter weather. The signal box above Outhgill in Mallerstang was overblown with snow driven by gales that howled along the flanks of Wild Boar Fell. Bill Hinman manned the first box, constructed in 1876. A replacement box was necessary with the introduction of double-track working. In 1934 the signalman struggling from Outhgill up the hillside to the box had to cope with a 19ft snowdrift. The snowplough sent to clear the tracks was derailed and the steam crane sent to recover it was snow-clogged; by daybreak only the tip of the crane's jib was visible. Signalmen entered the box by slithering down the massive drift.

During the inter-war years gangs of railwaymen worked on the permanent way, 60ft lengths of rail being manhandled. A substantial re-laying job was undertaken using 'rail-dogs', or scissor-like clamps. A score of men would lift a rail with the 'dogs' and a larger team would load them on to wagons. Men with picks and shovels re-ballasted the track. Bill Wilson of Appleby, ganger with

100 *A survey party illustrated in F.S. Williams' history of the Midland Railway.*

101 *Constructing Ormside viaduct, in the Eden Valley.*

the Extra Gang for many years until his retirement in the late 1920s, employed brains as well as brawn when the engine of a ballast train was derailed in the main line crossover at Crosby Garrett. Using a stack of fish plates as a fulcrum, he employed a 30ft rail as a lever to slip the engine back into place. Railway work was ill-paid and chancy. The penny-pinching Midland might dispense with the services of a man towards the end of December and re-hire him in early January, thus avoiding the payment of holiday entitlement.

102 *Long Meg viaduct under construction. Piers were sunk in the Eden.*

103 *Crosby Garrett station.*

104   *Staff at Crosby Garrett, in the heyday of the Settle-Carlisle.*

The run-down of the line occurred in the 1960s. Small stations were closed and concern was voiced by British Rail about the poor state of Ribblehead Viaduct. When it seemed likely that the line would be closed, or possibly privatised, there were lively local and national campaigns for its retention. The line was saved, the viaduct restored, and today the passenger service is popular. The Settle-Carlisle is also used for the transportation of gypsum to Kirkby Thore and coal from the southern hemisphere, which is conveyed by big ships to the Clyde and moved by rail to the power stations of South Yorkshire and the Midlands.

At Long Meg gypsum mine, the 'blue cobble' in which the gypsum was encased was ignored until, during the Second World War, several industrial companies banded together to exploit it. From sidings associated with the Settle-Carlisle line, over a period of around twenty years, about two million tons of 'blue cobble' were transported to a plant at Widnes. Since the Long Meg mine closed the land has been reclaimed by birch trees. In contrast, a stretch of the South Tynedale Railway, from Alston to Kirkhaugh, is a popular tourist attraction. Visitors who travel on England's highest narrow-gauge line, which is managed, maintained and operated by the volunteers of a preservation society, cross the splendid Gilderdale Viaduct.

Chapter 13

Farm Life

In medieval times open fields were divided into strips and cultivated with the help of ox-hauled ploughs. Strip lynchets near Wharton Hall and elsewhere show which hillsides were cultivated for cereal crops. In the Norse period, land near a settlement was known as *inbye* and the rough fell grazing for cattle and sheep was the *outgang*. Everitt, in his *Agrarian History of England*, recorded the average prices paid for stock at Kirkby Stephen in 1353: oxen were valued at 12s. 3d. a head; you might buy a good horse for 16s. 4d.; cows were 9s. 6d., wethers 1s. 3d. and pigs 2s. 6d. per head.

At Hutton-in-the-Forest, in Inglewood, a 17th-century dovecote and fishponds provided fresh food in lean times. Birds entered by the lantern in the centre of the roof, and from a ladder on a central pole (or 'potence') a man could reach into each of the 400 nesting boxes with which the walls were lined. Deer in the park were not just ornamental, for here was a ready supply of fresh meat in winter, much more appetising than the salted variety.

The Howards of Corby Castle were pioneer agriculturalists. In 1752 Philip Howard had a field sown with clover to demonstrate the value of 'artificial' grass. Three years later, turnips were being planted to improve the rotation of crops and provide good feed for farm stock in winter. The weight of turnips varied between 12 and 25lb. Almost ten years later, Philip Howard's example was followed by a Mr Collins of Wetheral and soon there were many disciples.

Between 1770 and 1830 the enclosure movement was under way. Vast tracts of land were brought into arable cultivation or, after being drained and improved, became pastureland for cattle and sheep. Water-powered mills turned locally grown cereals into oatmeal and provender. One standing where Cairn Beck joins the Eden near Warwick Bridge exemplified the transitional mill, embodying features from various periods. Its story was related to me by Bob Willis, the miller. Once owned by Corby Castle, it served as the manorial mill. The wheel revolved in a bed cut out of solid rock, a cast-iron breast wheel having been made in Carlisle in 1843. Upstairs was a pair of shelling stones, as well as a pair of oatmeal stones fashioned from Lazonby sandstone. Pairs of French 'burrs', or grinding stones, had been covered with an emery compound and dressed in the Sussex way.

With the break-up of the feudal system, the agricultural worker was free to barter his labour for wages. Hiring fairs as featured in the novels of Thomas Hardy were still operating in Cumbria after they had died out in the south. The heyday of the hirings was in the late 19th century, when an inexperienced 14-year-old lad who had left home clad in a new suit tramped to the nearest fair to stand with straw in mouth, indicating his availability for work. If taken on, he would serve for six months at an agreed price, which was no more than £4 for a new starter, although board and lodging were included. Carlisle had a hiring fair as late as 1949, as testified by Charles R. Denton, a correspondent in *Cumbria* who attended the event on Whit Saturday: 'Even this fair was a ghost of the former hirings. A few agreements were made between farmers and workers. Labour was scarce and few men and girls were seeking to be hired. Full employment in urban areas during the post-war period had stimulated the drift from the land that began after the war.'

In Victorian times, most people never strayed far from home and their lives were steeped in legend and superstition. Thomas Gibson wrote in 1887 that anyone hearing a cock crow before the house might expect a stranger to appear. If a piece of coke flew out of the fire, a coffin was implied. A mote in the wick of a candle was a sure sign that a letter was on the way. In the village of Winton, near Kirkby Stephen,

105 *A dale country farm hearth photographed in 1900.*

an old man with a belief in witches wore a hare's foot on one side of his beaver hat and on the other side a piece of bark or leaf from a rowan tree. No one would remove from one house to another on a Friday, for it was 'Friday flit, short sit.'

Home life for most was grim. Daniel Scott, in *Bygone Cumberland and Westmorland* (1899), commented on the almost total absence of ventilation and the insanitary conditions which meant that fevers were common. The staple items in the diet were oatcake and brown bread. Clothes were home-made and plain: 'hodden grey' (undyed wool) for the men and correspondingly good wear for the ladies. Clogs were worn by all classes, from parson down to the poorest labourer. Housewives had a curious method of preserving a stocking's heels, smearing them with melted pitch and then dipping them in the ashes of turf, a glutinous mixture that formed a compound both hard and flexible.

Up to the First World War, servants abounded at farms and larger houses. They were hired for the half-year at Whitsuntide and Martinmas, receiving a shilling to fix the appointment. Servant lasses, costing next to nothing, had to be content with board and lodging. To some they were little better than 'slaves and skivvies', but most were treated with kindness. Those from poor homes quickly responded to the improved living conditions.

A 'sarvant lass' who began a career of drudgery on a Westmorland farm in August 1904 packed her clothes in a paper parcel and was impressed by the size

106 *The cheerless kitchen of a Cumbrian farmhouse, around 1850.*

107 *Knitting sticks. On was worn in a leathern belt so that an extra needle might be used.*

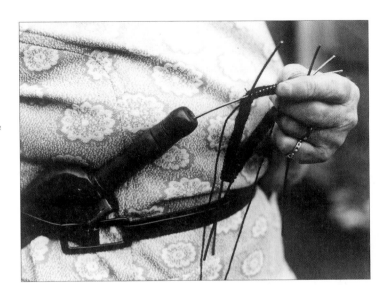

108 *Hand-knitting was widely practised in the upper dale to eke out limited incomes. The dagger-like sheath accommodated one of four metal needles.*

of the farmhouse. There was 'a sarvant lass elder than me' who 'git ma in t'way o' t'work'. (Tuition was given by an older girl.) Each morning and evening, the servant lass would collect a 'swill' (basket) and transport from the peat-house sufficient pieces to fill a 'bacon box'. Six months later, having been paid an agreed sum in gold sovereigns but seeking more varied experience, she 'hired to another spot'. There was scarcely any free time. Sometimes, having finished the necessary jobs by six o'clock on Sunday, she would be allowed out – until nine.

Spring-cleaning was an especially busy time, the walls of the farm outbuildings being white-washed and the flags 'scrubbed oot'. Butter-making and feeding calves on oilcake porridge, morning and night, were among the regular jobs on a farm. Washing was done on Monday, the clothes being washed, dried and ironed the same day. On baking day, a servant girl's special job was 'kneadin' t'bread' and 'peelin' apples fer pasties', as well as filling a large tin with ginger-bread. An almost unvarying diet took in hot-pot, rice pudding and apple tart. Oatmeal was the basis of porridge and haverbread, the last-named made on a 'bakstone' and put in a big 'kisk' (pot). There was never time to be 'stoad' (tired or bored).

Barbara Smith, writing in *Cumbria* about life at Bewcastle, to the north of Carlisle, recalled that all the dwellings had the right to cast peat from a specified peat-moss, which, since many of the farms and cottages were isolated, was better than carting coals from a distant railway station. About the year 1900, when game was plentiful, it provided food for large families or was sold to game dealers. As Barbara's father said, 'There was plenty for the gentry, plenty for the poachers and plenty for the vermin.' Sea trout and salmon were being caught by fair means and foul. A local blacksmith would surreptitiously make a 'liester', or fishing spear.

Jossie Atkinson, whom I visited at Cumpstone Hill, a farm near the head of Mallerstang, in 1984, had moved there with his family in 1930 and spent most of his time in a kitchen-cum-living room. In retirement he kept a few sheep and hens, his only companion being a dog. In the period just before the First World War a dale-country farmhouse did not have carpets on the ground floor; this was scrubbed every Saturday, the person with the brush working on hands and knees. A hearthrug might be laid each evening.

109 *Jossie Atkinson of Cumpstone Hill, Mallerstang in the kitchen of his remote farm.*

The huge fireplace incorporated an oven and boiler that was especially useful at pig-killing time when large quantities of hot water were required. A kettle hung from a 'reckon', the metal arm of which was capable of being swung to a position above the fire. A cupboard set in the wall near the fireplace was used for keeping medicines, some for humans, some for stock. A former housekeeper had used the oven for cooking beef and baking Christmas loaf and pasties of various kinds. The fuel was local peat, augmented with a little coal. Jossie had not cleaned the chimney for years, but he used to climb onto the roof of the house and drop down the flue a sled rope with a stone as a weight which he then attached to a sack filled with hay or bracken. When the bottom of the chimney had been blocked off, the sack was pulled up and down a few times, displacing the soot.

Coming from a family which combined farming with building, Jossie was an expert drystone waller. He remembered when hired shepherds tended flocks on gaited pastures, a gait representing the pasturage of a single sheep in an area of bog and rock where the term acre was meaningless. His brother Jack could 'mek a clog sole and then mek a pair of clogs', a popular form of footwear in 'clashy' weather. 'Clogs had iron caulkers at t'bottom and could be awk'ard things if it come snow. You'd be walking along on lumps of hard-packed snow.' They were usually worn when the farmer was at the peat workings.

Jossie 'fetched' peat in a 'coup', a large sled with wooden sides. 'Peats were grand on baking day; they were

110   *Milking a cow, as demonstrated at a special event in Appleby.*

terribly hot. If there was a lile bit o' red in t'bottom of your fire, and you broke a peat up, it started off practically right away.' Jossie went to a hill-end pit in Cotterdale for coal. Bogeys were used to transport coal from the mine to the horse-drawn cart of the customer, the cost per cartload being about 3s. 6d. Cotterdale coal, being small, was poured on to a hot peat fire and allowed to cake. 'Then you had to stab it wi' t'poker.'

Most farmers kept a pig that was larger and fatter than those in favour today. Jossie killed lots of pigs during the Second World War and, using the peat-fired oven, rendered down fat that was 'worth more than t'bacon to t'owd folk … long sen it was all dipping into t'frying pan wi' slices o' bread'. The 'proven' (feeding stuffs) were delivered in hessian bags and the sacks were retained for holding peat. Jossie's old Westmorland farmhouse had a 'beef baulk', from which a leg of beef was suspended and dried by the fire. The beef, being salted, could be kept for a considerable period.

Jossie used to 'hing' (hang) some hams in the baulk. A Grisedale man he knew 'butched' (slaughtered) on a grand scale. In November he kept about a hundred 'wether hoggs' (castrated sheep) which he fed liberally. He butched six hoggs every Monday morning, taking the meat to Hawes market.

111   *J.T. Hall of Murton takes his first crop of lambs to Murton Pike.*

At some Eden Valley farms a lad might spend a couple of hours after supper grooming horses and was roused from his sleep at 7 a.m. to fodder them before the start of another working day. Almost every village had its smithy, details of which were supplied to me by John Kirkpatrick when I visited Morland in 1954. John had been apprenticed to Richard Coates, who worked him 7 a.m. to 6 p.m. and paid him a shilling every Saturday. His wage rose by a shilling a year until he was a qualified smith. Before the First World War a good horse was valued at between £40 and £50 but wartime conditions elevated the price to around £100. The most popular breed was the Clydesdale which, having little hair on its legs, did not collect as much dirt as the Shires. John Kirkpatrick worked the smithy at Morland for 48 years, at one time attending well over a hundred horses. Mechanisation on the land caused the number to dwindle, so that in 1953 he shoed just one horse. Happily, he and his son had already invested in a garage.

On the North Pennines, farmer-miners thrived with the lead industry. A patchwork of hay meadows, their borders defined by drystone walls and open moorland beyond, extended as far as the eye could see. Generations of indomitable fell farmers kept cattle and sheep, mainly sheep, each flock hefted to its natal area. Westmorland extended eastwards to Birkdale, between the Upper Tees and Dufton, where there were two farms: an upper house from where, in the inter-war years, the Masons keepered Dufton Fell for the Appleby Castle Estate, and a lower farm belonging to the Tarn family of Middleton-in-Teesdale. In an early reference to Birkdale, John Dent was fined a shilling at Appleby in 1749. He had been exposing unwholesome meat. Thomas Raine, in a ballad about John Allison and Will Ritson, two local shepherds, written early in the 19th century, noted:

And Birkdale – it stands nigh the moor,
Is known the country round.
They live by keeping flocks of sheep;
They've got no tillage ground.

Walter White, the writer, visiting Birkdale in 1858, asked a local man how many sheep he considered fair stock to the acre. The answer was, 'Eh mon, ye begin at wrong end. Ye should ask how many ackers till a sheep.' When an old lady died at Birkdale, I was told when visiting this remote farm, her body was strapped to the back of a pony and the sorrowing party headed to the parish church at Dufton for the funeral service. Arriving early, they tethered the pony, with the body still attached, and sought the warmth and liquid comfort of a local inn. The pony slipped its halter and returned to the farmhouse, where children, noticing its reappearance, cried, 'Granny's coming back!'

112   *Birkdale Farm, in Westmorland's share of the upper valley of the Tees.*

My memories of Birkdale date from the 1950s, when the remaining farm was the home of the Bainbridge family. Sharing the high grazings near Birkale were sheep from some East Fellside farmers, at Hilton and Dufton. In 1962 the Bainbridges started the winter with some 400 ewes. They were still in the process of building up the flock. Then a blizzard raged until all they could see from the house was an undulating white desert. In the clear, sunny, bitterly cold days that followed three-quarters of the flock perished. That springtime,

113   *North Pennine sheep farmer, whose home was Birkdale.*

114 *A ewe of the popular Swaledale breed with twin lambs.*

Mary Bainbridge recalled, there was an unnatural quietness about Birkdale. The surviving sheep were too weary to bleat.

Historically, Scotch black-faced sheep grazed open common land. Subsequently, farmers crossed the sheep with Swardles (Swaledales), but shrewdly 'crossed back' with the Scotch type every fifth year to keep the breed hardy. Fifty years ago the Mallerstang flocks ranged in number from eighty to three hundred. Hellgill Farm, owned by T.W. Cleasy of Sedbergh, was one of those where a specific number of sheep were bound by agreement to remain on the farm, thus preserving the heaf-going instinct that in the absence of field boundaries meant they kept to specific areas. The Hellgill agreement meant that two hundred Swaledale ewes and sixty hoggs were permanently 'on the staff'.

Wether (castrated) lambs were sold off in the autumn as 'stores' and went to the lowlands to be fed up before being butchered. Most of the 'gimmers' were retained for breeding purposes. The 'drafts', those sheep that had produced four crops of lambs on the hills, were sold to lowland farmers to be cross-bred with mutton strains. A cross with a Wensleydale tup produced the popular Masham strain. Farmers in the Craven district used to hire a special train in winter to transport sheep on the Settle-Carlisle line to the Eden Valley farms, where they might subsist on root crops.

When cattle-rustling was rife along the border, a hardy black breed known as the Galloway was coveted. A Galloway was 'thrifty', able to survive on what it could find on the fell, plus a little hay. Its shaggy coat turned the worst of the weather. Calving took place in the spring and calves were dropped in autumn. Until the enclosure awards took effect in 1850, livestock was grazed on Langwathby Moor, where there was no fence or wall. A common Parish Bull was used for all breeds of cattle until after mid-century, when the selective breeding of livestock was practised.

Butter, not milk, left the little farms. A butter market was held at the Cloisters fronting both Appleby and Kirkby Stephen churches, where the start of trade was marked by the ringing of a butter-bell. Some Langwathby farmers took most

115   *The springtime sheep fair at Tan Hill was attended by farmers from Westmorland and Yorkshire.*

116   *Tan Hill sheep fair.*

117   *Sheep wintering on roots in the Eden Valley.*

118   *Butter-making appliances: sycamore bowl, Scotch hands and prints used to distinguish the produce of one farm from that of another.*

of their butter to Penrith, standing the market on a Tuesday. The old method of butter-making was to separate the cream by allowing milk to settle in bowls for the time taken by three meals – morning, night and the following morning – before skimming took place. On some farms shallow metal troughs called 'leads' were used, a stopper being removed to permit the 'blue' milk to drain away.

The cream was stored in a crock until churning day. Each week in summer there would be two churnings, with perhaps 60lb of butter made at a time. One churning sufficed in winter. End-over-end churns were operated and the length of time taken for the transformation to take place varied but was especially long in summer. The farm folk reckoned that a quart of cream equalled one pound of butter. When the butter had formed, the wooden cork was removed from the churn and the butter milk was allowed to drain away; it was fed to young stock – or poured on the porridge of the farm labourers! Clean, cold water was poured in and, especially in summer, a little salt added to the water to keep the temperature of the water down. A butter worker was used to squeeze water from the butter, then it was salted and rolled again.

Afterwards Scotch Hands, or small wooden bats, were used to pat the butter, weighed in pats of one pound or half a pound, into an appropriate shape and to place a design on top. This made the butter distinctive, the peculiar quality depending largely on which local herbage the cows had grazed. A purchaser was keen to known the source. Samuel Wood of Langwathby told me in the summer of 1954, when there was a flush of milk, that a pound of butter was worth as little as eight pence.

For many years, the Shorthorn was the main cattle breed of the upper Eden, being durable and dual-purpose, suitable for milk and beef. It thrived on 'poorish' ground. Before the fashion for de-horning cattle when young, this breed had quite long horns. In the 18th century, the 'short horned kind' of cattle were found mainly to the east of the Pennines, but they succeeded the longhorn breed on dairy farms in about 1820.

The Dales Shorthorn, which descended from improved stock, was tough, yielding a milk rich in butter-fat and ideal for butter-making or rearing calves. Shorthorns came in white and red forms, a blend of the two – known as a roan – being especially popular with dale farmers. In the 1880s, a white Shorthorn bull from the upper dale became the supreme champion at the Royal Show in Carlisle.

A decline of the breed was linked, in the minds of some breeders, with the governmental introduction of a licensing scheme for bulls. In 1935 the Shorthorn was still the most popular breed, having 19,908 licensed bulls compared with 1,210 of the Friesian, which was introduced from the Low Countries. With the demand for more milk, the Shorthorn was for a time crossed with the Ayrshire breed from south-west Scotland. During the industrial slump of the 1930s, an East Fellside farmer walked two young Shorthorn cows to market at Penrith, a distance of 10 miles, and was disheartened when they sold for a modest £16 10s. and £17.

Enthusiasts for the old type of Shorthorn, meeting at Penrith in January 1944, formed the Northern Dairy Shorthorn Society. The Dent family, of Winton near Kirkby Stephen, remained faithful to the breed in changing times. G.W. Dent of Wharton Hall had been one of the founders of the Northern Dairy Shorthorn Breeders' Association. His son, George Alderson Dent, moved from Wharton to Winton House in 1962, taking with him 20 cows and 40 hoggs. The cows were the foundation of what became an impressive Shorthorn herd.

119   *Longhorn cattle, superseded on dale country farms by the gentle Shorthorn.*

The evolution of the Dairy Shorthorn stock at Winton House is recorded in *Coates's Herd Book*, the oldest register of its type in the world.

Fellside farmers in the upper Eden Valley valued their independence. In the days before veterinary surgeons were widely available, a cupboard set in a wall near the fire was a repository for 'all sorts o' bits o' things', including bottles of sheep medicine. Jossie Atkinson knew precisely what to do if a ewe found lambing difficult. He would visit the luckless animal with some 'lambing oil'. He had bottled a tablespoonful of turpentine and a tablespoonful of water, and this he poured down the sheep's throat. 'I never had one that festered.' If a cow calved but did not 'clean', or part with the afterbirth, within five or six hours, Jossie would wait for a full day then mix a tablespoonful of saltpetre into a pint of cream, pouring this into the cow horn he used when dosing stock. He administered it 'at t'cow mouth' and 'in an hour or two you'd see that cleansing come. If it didn't just shift it, you had to give it another dose, twelve hours after. But it nearly always worked first time.'

The railway was a boon to farmers who had to deliver farm stock at a distance. Jossie recalled the time, in about 1915, when no fewer than 365 spring bullocks about six months old and some geld cows were trucked at Hawes railway junction for Richmond Moor, where a fair was held in November. Old Will Pratt of Garsdale would entrain at Hawes Junction – the old name for Garsdale station

– to buy cattle in Scotland and, of course, have them delivered by rail, which had now removed the need for cattle droving.

Jim Monkhouse, writing about the farming operations at Langwathby in the 1930s, observed that the 21 small to medium-sized farms of 1850 had been reduced to ten. By the late 1990s there were seven. With horses still operating in 1932, about forty men, including the farmers and their families, were needed to work the local farms. A labourer received about 38 shillings a week, with the possibility of more if overtime were worked at a rate of 8d. per hour. Single men, hired at Whitsuntide (May) and Martinmas (November), were paid between £28 and £35 per period, board and lodging being provided.

In those inter-war years, a local farmer might freely graze his stock on the village green, which was covered with cow-claps to the dismay of local lads who wished to play football. Farming arable land followed the set pattern of a six-year rotation, land nearest the homestead being kept as a cow pasture for convenient milking next morning. In-wintered cattle were fed on hay, straw and turnips carried in 'swills', or baskets.

120   *Hannah Hauxwell of Low Birk Hatt at her remote North Pennine home. She farmed single-handedly in Baldersdale and became a television celebrity.*

With the price for milk rising, protein cake fed to the cows stimulated production, a process that began when Express Dairy at Appleby consigned Eden Valley milk to London by rail. The hand-milking of cattle would begin at 6 a.m. With the opening of the Settle-Carlisle railway in the 1870s, some farmers sent milk in 10 or 12 gallon kits to Bradford and Leeds, but this was a chancy business for they were not always paid. Jim recalled that a newly calved cow sold at Penrith auction mart on a Tuesday in the 1930s had to be of top quality to be worth £30. A cow might lose condition if walked to market, so the best animal would be transported in a horse-drawn bull cart. After about 1932, a motor lorry was available to carry two cows at a time.

'Mashed haver', that is oats, rolled flat, was fed to the beef stock. Jim recalled it had to be mixed with some linseed and cotton cake. Delivered to the farm in slab form, it was put through a hand-operated cake crusher. Silcocks brought out a 'fattening cake' to replace this method of feeding. Haytime on an Eden Valley stock farm during the time when horse power was employed to do the

121 *Bill Robson, Edenvale farmer and prominent local naturalist who lived at New Hall, near Appleby, photographed at High Cup Nick on the North Pennines.*

heaviest work began towards the end of July and, in poor weather conditions, might well last into September. Mowing was a job for the early morning. Grass cut slightly better when moist with dew and, this being the coolest part of the day, it was most comfortable for a working horse.

In unpredictable weather, the hay might be kept for a short time in 'foot cocks', small heaps made with deft use of rake and foot. Larger heaps were called 'pikes'. Spread out again, it was forked on to the cart, which was them 'kemmed', or combed, to remove loose strands of hay and taken to the barn. At harvest time, a field was opened up by scythe to enable the horse-drawn machine to be used. Sheaves were stacked into 'stooks' to keep them dry whenever rain was in prospect. After they had dried out, they were accommodated in a Dutch barn or a large stack was made. On threshing days, several farmers would join forces, each providing several men to make up the labour force of eight or so necessary to operate a threshing machine.

When the thresher was due, a stack of coal and copious supply of water was laid in. The hardest job was carrying sacks of grain, each weighing up to 20 stone, up the granary steps into storage. The farmers' wives and daughters worked just as hard as the men since it was expected that each day three or four meals would be provided for the dozen labourers. Old-time writers mentioned a summer spectacle, the 'harvest glow', and Eden is still 'the golden vale'. With the outbreak of the Second World War, mechanisation led to a phasing out of horses and the use of tractors. On the hill farms, the sure-footed fell pony was succeeded by the 'li'l grey Fergie', the Ferguson tractor that was handy and low-geared enough for work on sloping ground. Latterly, quads, the all-terrain vehicles, have become common; they travel at speed across field and fell, the dog riding pillion.

Farmers began selling their milk in the 1930s. At the dalehead it was conveyed in kits to Libby's factory at Milnthorpe. At the same time Express Dairy established their depot at Appleby, which for many years provided dairy farmers over a wide area with a reliable outlet. In 1929, when a senior official of the Dairy visited

122   *A Land Car, adapted from a standard model, has been set to work mowing meadow grass.*

123   *Horse-and-sled haytime.*

124   *Tractor and baling machine speeds up haytime.*

the Eden Valley, he represented the largest distributor of milk in London and other major cities. A week later another representative visited Carlisle to survey the land and she returned a week later for further inquiries. In April 1930 the chairman, Titus Barham, paid his first visit to the area, approaching by way of bleak Stainmore. He wrote to John Crosby, of Kirkby Thore, who was keen to see the dairy established, 'I have noticed the mountains and not one green blade of grass have I seen. In my opinion this is no place to put down a dairy.' Barham changed his mind when he was shown the verdant Eden Valley.

Construction began the same year and despite a stormy winter the main structure was erected by the springtime. Trials were held over the summer. By autumn 1931 the Express Dairy's Appleby depot was in full production, with John Crosby's son Richard its first manager. In the early days milk was transported to London in special milk tanks lined with glass, each capable of holding 3,000 gallons. At first, the tankers were attached to the train that left Appleby at 3.26 p.m. As farmers became more confident of the new scheme and milk production on the farms rose, a special train was arranged. It took six tanker-wagons northwards to Carlisle, where they were attached to a train that also served Nestles. The combined load was transported speedily to the metropolis and was on the doorsteps of Londoners or in retail shops early the following day. Appleby also consigned fresh farm eggs to London. Among those received were some, usually brown, which were too large for normal handling. They were set in attractive cartons and marketed as Eden Valley Eggs. At the

125   *Appleby Creamery. The train made a daily run to London with milk.*

peak period, just before the Second World War, the weekly total of eggs collected was 1,224,000.

The rationalisation of milk distribution in the 1950s determined that it had to be sold locally, so it was decided at Appleby to make it into Cheddar cheese. This led to the opening in 1971 of what was then the most modern Cheddar cheese plant in Europe. By its 50th anniversary the creamery was employing 190 people. Blue tankers were being driven daily to 400 farms lying between Stainmore and Ullswater, including Mallerstang. The supply of milk was 385,000 litres a day, of which 345,000 litres were being used for the production of cheese. The remaining 40,000 litres were transported to other depots for bottling or processing.

Livestock, once traded in the main street of a town like Kirkby Stephen, was now sold through auction marts, several important ones being found in the Eden Valley. Kirkby Stephen is noted for its sales of Swaledales, with tups now reaching astronomically high prices. John Kidd, an auctioneer associated with Penrith Farmers and Kidd's, was a forceful man who was hard on anyone who did not pay his dues, even saying 'Go to my office and get paid up' if he met them in the street. Carlisle is also an important marketing centre.

Each auction mart has a café and in the small towns and villages dale country humour is evident. A waitress holding a plate of pie and peas at a lamb sale in Lazonby asked a farmer where he intended to sit, to which he replied, 'Anywhere, lass; I'll go to it.' It was, of course, a knife-and-fork meat, with a choice of peas and

126 *Hilton farmer and his fell pony.*

127 *The Dales pony, of the type bred for light shaft work, is now often used for trekking.*

salads. Other home-baked food included currant pasty, the filling being half an inch thick.

At the Lazonby lamb sale I attended in 1982, almost 16,000 lambs went through the ring and a good price was being realised. Lazonby advertised itself as 'the foremost grey-faced (mule) lamb centre'. Most of the lambs on offer had been reared on fell farms, above the 1,000ft contour line. In the 1930s this type of lamb was found within

128 *Two Eden Valley farmers wait to have a horse shod at an agricultural event, Appleby.*

a 15-mile radius of Alston. Breeders on Alston Moor had once driven their surplus stock on roads to Armathwaite, Langwathby and Lazonby, which were all sited on the Settle-Carlisle railway, but Lazonby's market developed because it was the nearest to the breeding area. Farmers used to walk the lambs, which was no easy matter if they had just been 'spained', or separated from the parent ewes. In some cases the journey was spread over two days. In the evening stock would be driven into the field of a friendly farmer, while the drover stayed overnight in the farmhouse.

The days when many Cumbrian farmers over-wintered hoggs on sea-washed turf, such as Burgh Marsh near the mouth of the Eden, are still within living memory. Sheep from the hill farms were driven home during the first week in April and the marsh was left to the wild birds until 1 May, when the summer stock arrived. This was mainly cattle, with a few ewes and their new lambs. The wintering sheep arrived in the first week in November. From time to time unexpectedly high water overswept the marshes, drowning scores and sometimes hundreds of sheep. Today, insurance considerations inhibit this custom. In the early 1970s, when I chatted with Bob Gate, a former 'herd' on Burgh Marsh, I was told that pasturage was controlled by a system of 'stints' apportioned among local users, one 'stint' equalling a beast, two 'stints' a mature horse or five sheep. At one time three herds were employed. Snowdon Armstrong, the best-known of them, carried out his duties from 1916 to 1929. His son Ernest, of West End Farm, served as reeve, or secretary, to the marsh committee.

The pattern of beef breeding underwent a profound change in the 1960s with the importation of the Charolais, the first of several continental breeds that were

129 *Sweeping up hay in the northern dale country.*

130 *A drystone waller repairing a gap above Smardale. The wall is two walls in one, held together by 'throughstones'.*

to appear on Cumbrian farms. By the 1980s, and contrary to earlier practice, most suckler cows were housed during the winter, only 11 per cent of hill herds wintering out of doors. Cubicle sheds enabled cows to be kept in dry, sheltered conditions, handy to the farmhouse at feeding time. In-wintering also led to a decline in the 'poaching', or hoof damage, caused by damp grassland. On most farms, haytime gave way to silage-time, the grass being taken in a wilted state. Nowadays a primary concern is the low price of milk.

Farmers' markets exist at Brough, Orton, Penrith and Pooley Bridge. At Brough, the venue is the Memorial Hall. Most of the farmers and producers live within thirty miles of the village. In addition to the usual range of meats and poultry, the products include venison, organic vegetables, cheese, cakes and jams. Farmers have become, in part, keepers of the landscape. A shift towards less intensive farming, and greater care of the countryside, is evident. Cumbria Farmer Network is a co-operative of over sixty farmers across the county who assist others to meet change and secure their futures and that of the area in which they farm.

Chapter 14

Natural History

T he River Eden is clean and species-rich, noted for its resident trout and migratory salmon. John Kirkbride, a 'modest tackle maker of Carlisle', penned *The Northern Angler* in 1832, when rod and line fishing was a novelty, listing the dressings he used when tying trout flies. The Carlisle Angling Association, at its inaugural meeting in the *Royal Oak* on 17 December 1852, proclaimed as its mission 'the better protection of the River Eden and its tributaries with a view to the preservation and increase of the fish therein and for the improvement of Angling in the District'. The appeal was directed mainly at the affluent, angling being beyond the means of the poor. With poaching rife, full-time watchers were recruited, tempted by the grant of free tickets. A device known as 'The Jack', consisting of hooks attached to a line that was floated out into the river, was banned for being an unsporting way of fishing. After pondering on the wisdom of allowing salmon roe to be used as trout bait, the committee decided that any roe used must have been obtained lawfully before the end of the season.

Fishing rights on the lower Eden were originally exercised using nets and traps. The lords of the manor of tidal reaches allowed their tenants to buy the right to use a boat. On higher reaches of the Eden, the owners of adjoining land claimed the fishing rights, and over the years many such rights, which included access to the river among the conditions, were sold separately from the rights to the land.

Early in the year Atlantic salmon, having grown sleek and fat feeding in deep waters between Greenland and Iceland, return to their natal rivers on a spawning run. Haaf-net fishermen and men operating with nets from boats intercepted those heading for the River Eden. At Rockcliffe, sixty and more years ago, fishing took place on a shift basis so that every hour of day and night was worked. A night's haul might be four or five cartloads. Most of the catch was consigned to London but many fine fish ended up in local larders.

Four men fished the mouth of the Eden by day and four by night, the change of shifts occurring at six o'clock. Salmon were allowed unhindered passage from 6 a.m. on Saturday morning until midnight on Sunday. E.R. Burnett wrote

131 *Salmon trap on the Eden at Corby, residence of Henry Howard.*

in *Cumbria* about 'Bob' of Glasson who, 'losing his return footing', landed on the Scottish shore and had to carry his great net back through Carlisle. His experience was not unique among the haaf-netters. Like many of his kind, Bob had a strong religious faith. He was a member of the congregation of one of the many Methodist chapels and after an evening service would go out to fish the incoming tide.

Haaf is Norse for sea, a haaf-net being fixed to a wooden frame 16 feet in length to form a pouch or bag, like a large shrimp net. The net was operated manually because an Act of Parliament of 1861 prohibited the catching of salmon in England with a fixed engine, except where rights were held by ancient charter, as in the case of some monasteries. The method was regarded by some as more ancient than effective. The nets I saw when visiting the Solway in 1978 had a beam of pine, with legs of greenheart, this wood having a good 'whip'. The frames were draped with nylon net, some men knitting their own. Any truncheon-like piece of wood, even part of a banister, was considered suitable for dispatching a netted salmon. In summer the net might become festooned with weed, one man who lifted his finding it decorated with hedge-trimmings. A fisherman might walk for three-quarters of an hour before reaching a good area for fishing and at night he relied on being able to see lights on the Scottish and English shores. Away to the east, a string of them marked the location of Kingmoor railway marshalling yard.

Boats used for salmon fishing had a length of about twelve feet and were five feet in the beam. A net some twelve feet deep and up to thirty or forty yards long was draped between bank and boat and the boat then worked round in a half circle. Men slew the salmon as nets were landed. Spawning fish were not taken. Known as 'old 'uns', and recognised immediately, they were allowed to swim free. Lord Lonsdale owned the rights, leasing them to Ormans of Carlisle and later to Thomas Robinson of Cargo. Fish over 30lb in weight were commonplace, and occasionally a salmon would make the scales dip at 40 to 50lb.

The extent of Rockcliffe Marsh varies according to the whims of river, tide and weather. Down the years, the Castletown estate managed the marsh wisely. Robert Mounsey, who became the prime mover at Rockcliffe, bought the estate and obtained the consent of the Earl of Lonsdale, lord of the manor, and the other commoners to enclose the manorial waste of some 2,000 acres, or half the parish. Near the marsh are two small cottages which were homes to the herds who rode on horseback and looked after the stock. Cattle found rich feeding on the salty acres and sheep wintered here avoided liver fluke by feeding on land periodically covered by salt water.

When Hutchinson compiled his monumental history of Cumberland in 1794, Rockcliffe was noted for its geese. In the 19th century, the commonest grey goose of the Solway was the bean goose, which breeds in Scandinavia and northern Finland and is the quietest of this group of birds. The commonest in recent times has been the pink-footed goose. Most of the overwintering pinkfoots nest in Iceland. Shooting geese from punts was a sport practised by Jackson Edgar and Billy Marsh of Rockcliffe. The craft, made of larch and bought second-hand from Gretna, had a length of about fourteen feet, and was two feet six inches in the beam. The punt-gunner lay full length in the boat. In his mouth was one end of a piece of string that was connected with the trigger of the gun. As soon as he came within range of the ducks, he yanked back his head and released the trigger. The ducks saw him, of course, but by the time the shot reached them they were at an ideal height above the water of a foot or eighteen inches. The gun had a bore of about two inches and the muzzle was packed with a quarter of a pound of blasting powder and eight or ten ounces of shot. The effect of the recoil was to send a punt backwards for eight or ten yards, but as many as 65 duck were killed by one shot.

132 *Whooper swans. A wintering herd of Icelandic swans have favoured fields near Temple Sowerby.*

Eddie Park and Archie Johnson, well-known wildfowlers, once lost their sense of direction on Solway sands and struck out in the hope of finding the marsh. Instead they encountered a foot high white line – the edge of the tide! Fortunately they knew the location of a large tree. Packs and guns were placed in the branches before the men climbed up and watched the grey waters swirl about them.

The Benedictines of Wetheral may have created islands to ensure a good number of salmon entered their coops. The art was to build coops on one side of an island and ensure the river was fairly shallow on the other since salmon tend to make for the strongest current, their shape and muscular arrangement being ideal for lusty forward propulsion. Those entering the coop passed through a limited space and could not normally find their way back. Trapped, they were collected from above.

Fifty years ago James McNeil, who lived at Wetheral, told me of his life on the lower Eden as a ghillie. A wise angler used greased lines, with Merry Widow and Butcher as favourite flies. James rowed anglers about the river and kept a gaff and net handy to recover any salmon that were hooked and brought to the boat. Fifteen boats were moored along the bank for the salmon season and the average weight of a fish was 16lb. James said a Chester-le-Street angler was credited with landing a fish weighing 45½lb, a record for spring fish. An autumn record was recorded by a Liverpool man whose salmon made the scales dip at 56lb.

The Eden surges through gorges at Lazonby and Wetheral. 'Toffs' arrived at Lazonby from Bradford and Leeds to stay at the *Brackenbank Hotel*, which became the base for their angling excursions. Having caught the early morning train, the men were met by ghillies and taken on the river in boats. They fished the day through. A man would keep one salmon but any others were despatched to Edwards and Walden in London, their name appearing on the special boxes in which the salmon were transported.

The Eden has major tributaries, including Eamont and Lowther, Lyvennet and Petteril, and Gelt and Irthing close to the Scottish border. Each contributes something of its own character to the changing nature of fishing on the Eden. Until the 1960s, the river had England's finest run of spring salmon. In common with many other rivers of the North Atlantic numbers have declined, but many fish are caught from mid-March when the first serious run arrives. The main run of salmon in the Eden occurs in the 'spring', the run actually beginning in January, but lesser runs take place in summer and autumn.

The fish which tipped the scales at 56lb was caught in the Warwick Hall water in November 1892. (The current British record is 64lb, the salmon being hooked in the River Tay in 1922.) The current guide to the river, published by Eden Council, describes as 'by far the prettiest of the salmon fishing' the reach downstream from Waters Meet (where the Eamont joins the Eden) to Wetheral: 'Within this, perhaps the most spectacular is below the sandstone cliffs and ancient woodlands of the Lazonby Gorge.' A steadily increasing number of sea

133 *The dipper finds its food on the bed of a fast-flowing beck.*

134 *Lapwing, a bird of moist places that winters on the coast.*

trout accompanies the salmon runs and the Eden has a growing reputation for the fish. With plenty of cover and gravel beds, the tributaries are ideal for brown trout, which are abundant but do not usually grow very large. The upper Eden offers wild trout fishing at its best.

Eden is primarily a game fish river but it also holds a good number of grayling, chub and dace. Edgar Cave, detailing the history of the Carlisle Angling Association in around 1978, commented, 'For decades, these have been regarded as vermin, inimical to the well-being of the game fish and locally referred to rather contemptuously as skellies.' Grayling fishing may be productive downstream from Musgrave, the fish being tempted with small Treacle Parkin and Red Tag flies. Until 1880, however, the grayling was not found in the Eden. The river had escaped the grayling-stocking fever of Victorian times. Then Christopher D. Thompson of Seaton Carew, Durham (1848-1905), who frequented the higher reaches during the trout season and fished for the grayling on the Ure with equal enthusiasm, released a tank of fry, tipping them from a milk churn over the churchyard wall at Great Musgrave and into the river. He was assisted in this by George Alderson. For a while it seemed that the experiment had not succeeded but the pioneer grayling were breeding in the deeper water around Ormside and Appleby.

In the following years the grayling population expanded downstream. By 1890 they were at Kirkby Thore and six years later they were represented in the Winderwath water to well below Culgaith. They also made themselves at home in the lower reaches of such tributaries as Lyvennet, Crowdundle and Marton Becks. Among the 'grayling greats' was William Nelson who, according to

135 *An oystercatcher nesting on riverside shingle.*

research by John Austin, was born in Paradise Cottage, Appleby in 1862, and is best known for his charming book *Fishing in Eden* (1922). Nelson was originally apprenticed in Appleby to a cabinet maker, but in the late 1880s he got himself through college and became headmaster of the Royal School for the Deaf in Manchester. It was probably in this city that he first met Arthur Ransome, who wrote an angling column for the *Manchester Guardian*. He and Nelson became firm friends and visited Appleby many times in pursuit of grayling.

The otter has returned to the Eden and its flute-like whistle is heard in the gloaming. Among the riverside bird life, the oystercatcher has a nesting tenancy where the river is passes through stony areas. On the high Pennines bird life is sparse but exciting. W.H. Palmer and friends, ascending Cross Fell on a nocturnal expedition from the top of Hartside Pass, roused cock grouse into explosive 'becks': 'Naturally, roosting among the heather at 2,500 feet above the sea, they had not expected the tramp of nailed boots close by them in the dusk.' The melancholy double-whistle of the golden plover is heard and I once found a nesting 'scrape' containing plover chicks at the edge of the plateau. The chicks were inconspicuous and inert, their down speckled with gold.

Dotterel feed up on their migratory journey from the shores of the Mediterranean to far northern nesting grounds, journeys flown at close quarters and with a chorus of whistles, and the species has bred intermittently on Cross Fell. Small and rather plump, with a mincing gait, the bird sits tightly on its clutch of eggs, unnoticed by enemies, protecting them with its body from the high Pennine chill. In 1785, when Carlisle medical practitioner John Heysham found a nest, he gave the first description of an egg of British origin.

When the gamekeeper ruled a moorland tract belonging to an estate only he and the farmer – with the keeper's permission – might visit the area during the nesting season. But moorland, once so quiet, is now over-run with sheep and people. Since the Second World War, when sheep numbers rose to help feed a beleaguered people, heather has been thinned by overgrazing and replaced in many cases by sheep-resistant Nardus grass.

From the eastern rim of Cross Fell's summit plateau one surveys the upper valley of the Tees and the Moor House National Nature Reserve, covering over 10,000 hectares of the Pennine moors between Cumbria and County Durham. The reserve is traversed by the Pennine Way. Wayfarers pass through a landscape of blanket bog and heather, cross-leaved heath and sphagnum moss, with contrasting outcrops of limestone. During the nesting season golden plover stand sentinel. The back of a bird, that likes bare, open ground, is golden-brown and speckled with black. The birds of the southern race are not so boldly black on the underparts as those which winter in Britain but nest far to the north. The warbling of skylarks is heard from high-flying birds that are mere dots against the scudding clouds. A meadow pipit draws attention to itself by descending like a shuttlecock, with stiff wings and tail, singing all the while.

The main reserve, at around 1,650 feet above sea level, consists of heather moorland, peat bogs and a few drier areas where bilberry and coarse-mat grass grow. Thyme, harebell and mountain pansy are found wherever limestone occurs. Near the Widdybank Fell nature trail are specimens of spring gentian, which in Britain occurs only in Teesdale and in western Ireland. Another botanical celebrity is the mountain everlasting, the closest British relative to edelweiss.

Cow Green Reservoir, in a shallow basin once rich in alpine flora, is at too high an altitude to appeal to birds at nesting time, though several species of duck and geese may sojourn here in winter. The reservoir was made, against much opposition from conservationists, to cater for an industrial demand lower down the Tees that never fully developed and the vast dam robbed a waterfall called Cauldron Snout of its appeal. It used to roar in isolation, like a prophet in the

136 *The Rev. G.K. Evens, better known as 'Romany', the naturalist who featured on BBC's Children's Hour, was a Methodist minister at Carlisle with angling and farming friends in the Eden Valley. He is pictured with his dog Raq.*

wilderness, water coursing down a natural staircase of Whin Sill to the confluence of Tees with Maize Beck beneath the hard grey face of Falcon Clints.

Upland birds seem fewer in number than they were. Happily, there have been fewer major landscape changes here than elsewhere. The North Pennines Area of Outstanding Natural Beauty has 40 per cent of Britain's upland hay meadows, usually wet fields noted for the richness of their wild plants and profusion of nesting birds. A leaflet issued to visitors to the region informs them that 80 per cent of the English population of black grouse is found here. On moorland, the merlin flies down larks and pipits, which remain relatively common.

For generations, the Renwick family made its mark on the North Pennines as shepherds, gamekeepers and wallers. An ever-restless family, its members worked on the Greenwich Hospital estate. Ivan Renwick, with whom I chatted in 1983, lived in a house at the end of a 'lonnin', or lane, that terminated at an elevation of 1,000 feet. A native of Garrigill, Ivan had a spell of work in lead mines, where he displayed an aptitude for turning stone arches and timbering levels as the miners drove further into a fell. In 1938, when living at Cumrew, he became under-keeper to Harry Potts on the Croglin Estate, being paid £2

137   *Romany's vardo or caravan was of the four-wheeled variety and is now preserved near his last home at Wilmslow in Cheshire.*

a week and provided with a house and a suit of clothes so he did not turn out on a shoot looking untidy.

The gamekeeper's job, as he knew it, was to eliminate birds and animals classified as 'vermin'. Heather was 'swizzened', or burnt in an organised way in strips, to get rid of old plants and encourage the growth of fresh shoots. Ivan's beat was at an elevation of around 2,000 feet, about level with Hartside Top. He knew the torments of the Helm Wind, which periodically frolicked along the East Fellside, 'knocking back' the growth of grass. Among the major changes in his long life was the coming of the tractor, its ruts having since 'riven to bits' many an old moorland track.

138 *A Pennine gamekeeper.*

139 *Ernest Blezard, for many years curator of the wildlife section of Tullie House, Carlisle.*

140 *A roe deer. The old British type survived on Solway Moss, whence it spread widely during the Second World War, using newly planted conifers for cover.*

Wild Boar Fell, which dominates Mallerstang, takes its name from the death at the hands of Sir Richard de Musgrave, a 15th-century dignitary, of the last boar in the district. After the Musgrave tomb in Kirkby Stephen church was opened in 1847, the wild boar's tusk found within was subsequently put on view in a glass case. A trial on a deer-stealing charge took place at Appleby in 1665 and the men who confessed to the deed were fined £20, in accord with the statute. Free-ranging deer inhabited the fells round Mallerstang until as late as 1725, the last deer-keeper living at Riddinghouse.

Two notable nature reserves are found along the disused Darlington-Tebay railway. Waitby Greenriggs reserve, a County Wildlife Site, is not far from Kirkby Stephen. The sloping bands of limestone and wetter track beds contain floral diversity, with over 200 species of flowering plant recorded here. Among the gems are bird's-eye primrose, autumn gentian and a variety of orchids. Further west, in Smardale, a designated National Nature Reserve, the landscape is spectacular and the croaking of ravens imparts a lonesome flavour. Here is one of only two breeding sites in England of the Scotch Argus butterfly. Flowers are profuse and varied and the mammalian residents include squirrels, roe deer and otters.

Kingmoor, not far from Carlisle city centre, is best known as a railway marshalling yard. It is also the name for a nature reserve established in 1913 to conserve woodland planted in the 18th century. In the mid-14th century, Edward III gave

141 *A fell-going fox drawn by Richard Clapham, who wrote several books on the Lake District.*

Kingmoor – then a tract of moorland – to the people of Carlisle for grazing and as a source of peat for fuel. In the grounds of Acorn Bank, a mansion near Temple Sowerby, the National Trust has a huge collection of medicinal and culinary herbs as well as walled orchards in which traditional varieties of fruit are grown. An unwelcome stranger, now well established along the banks of the Eden, is Himalayan balsam, big and fleshy, distributing its seeds by a spring device.

On the trembling landscape of Solway Moss, an area of heather and extensive peat workings, are red grouse. Visiting sportsmen have commented on their large size, the birds being much larger than their upland cousins, a benefit of the good feeding. Here, too, are roe deer of the old North British stock, darker than the deer in southern Lakeland that were affected when the reddish Austrian roe was introduced into the Windermere area in Victorian times. It was from Solway Moss, during and after the Second World War, that roe – using the cover of newly-planted forests – began to spread across the north west and regain their old habitats. Peter Delap of Appleby, a prominent member of the British Deer Society and an authority on roe, frequented the woods at Hoff, where he knew the deer as individuals, and imitated the gruff call of the testy resident buck.

Chapter 15

Modern Times

The administration of most of the Eden Valley is the concern of a district council, which has two offices in Penrith and thriving information centres at Kirkby Stephen and Alston. Eden, the second largest such district in England, covering 215,646 hectares and with a population of 52,000, is the most sparsely populated region in England and Wales. Around a fifth of it lies within the Lake District National Park and almost a quarter is within the North Pennines Area of Outstanding Natural Beauty. The local economy, resting largely on tourism, tends to specialise in consumer services and Eden is predominantly a 'small firm economy'.

Carlisle, the old county town of Cumberland and home to around 72,000 people, is now part of the City of Carlisle local government district, the administrative centre for both the district and county of Cumbria. In the not-so-distant days, Carlisle had affinities with Petra, the 'rose-red city half as old as time'. It was a joy to motor towards it on a sunny evening after a day spent by Solway Firth and to see the warm glow of red sandstone, an effect only spoiled in the 1960s by the new Civic Centre, a skyscraper of concrete and glass in historic Rickergate. The city was historically cut off from England proper by 'forty miles of sheep and Shap'. The main route south was the A6 to Penrith,

142 *Sketches of Old Penrith. From Penrith, Eden Council administers Edenvale and Alston.*

143   *Radio Cumbria is broadcast from Carlisle.*

but now the city is linked with the rest of England by the M6 motorway and with Glasgow and the north by the M74/A74. Carlisle is also the main station on the West Coast main railway line. The 'burring' speech of the folk has about it a little 'Scotch' when heard by southerners. The city has developed a strong life of its own, with good sporting links. Brunton Park Stadium, in the centre of the city, is the home of Carlisle United Football Club, which has played in all four divisions of English football. In the 1974-5 season the team went to the top of the old Division One.

Carlisle became an industrial city in the 19th and early 20th centuries, the Caldew Valley area seeing most of the development. Initially there were textile mills, engineering works and food manufacturers. Famous firms that were founded or had factories in Carlisle include Carr's of Carlisle (now part of United Biscuits), Metal Box (now part of Crown Cork and Seal), John Laing and the hauliers Eddie Stobart Ltd.

The city has a spacious central area, now a pedestrian precinct, where the Cross erected in 1682 (successor of a medieval market cross) stands. It is hallowed ground, being the focal point of the Roman settlement. From here, at 8 a.m. in late August, is proclaimed the Great Fair, now revived as an annual Festival, thus sustaining a custom that began in 1353. An area known as The Lanes, between Lowther Street and Scotch Street, is a modern shopping precinct sanctified by historical references, such as Three Canons Lane, Longcakes Lane, Friars Court and Globe Lane.

144 *Carlisle Town Hall as it was in 1780. The modern municipal centre is in a multi-storey building.*

The bold red sandstone towers of the Citadel are in view of the passengers leaving the railway station. The original Citadel was erected on the order of Henry VIII in 1541-3 to guard the southern approach. It was rebuilt as the Court Houses between 1810-21 to the design of Sir Robert Smirke. The pageantry of the High Court judge arriving for Carlisle Assizes accompanied by the High Sheriff of Cumberland took place for the last time in October 1971, ending a tradition that the city had known for about one thousand years. The ceremonial visit to the cathedral church by judge and officials of the court was a reminder of medieval times, when all important acts were preceded by prayers that true justice might be done. The spectacle offered by the Assize party was colourful. The Judge wore his scarlet robes and the High Sheriff was decked in ruffled shirt, velvet doublet and breeches, and wore the sword of justice. The Dean wore his traditional ecclesiastical garments, the Under Sheriff top hat and morning dress, and the Mayor his robes and chain of office. From the Cathedral the party moved to the Assize Courts, where the Judge was greeted by a fanfare of trumpets. Under the Courts Act of 1971, the Assizes, dating back to Norman times, were

145 *In summer it is not unusual to see a parked caravan, the horse taking advantage of a roadside flush of grass.*

replaced by a permanent Crown Court, and the Citadel towers now serve as offices for Cumbria County Council. The Cumbrian police headquarters were switched to the main street when, in January 2005, their former quarters were swamped by the worst flooding of the Eden since 1822.

A hint of ancient history is evident in some of the street names, English Street and Scotch Street reflecting the constantly shifting border status. Castle Street echoes the military past and Paternoster Row and Blackfriars Street recall medieval religion. The former was the main approach to the cathedral, the Blackfriars being a religious order who tended a medieval church. Lowther Street alludes to a Cumbrian family noted for their drive and money.

Names bestowed on the numerous public houses evoke the history and traditions of the locality. The coming of the railways was reflected in the naming of the *Royal Scot* and *Caledonian*. A medieval atmosphere might be detected in *Inglewood Forest* and *Robin Hood*. *The Arroyo Arms* commemorates one of the Crimean battles in which the Border Regiment figured. Robert Burns stayed at the *Malt Shovel*. The landlord of the *Museum Inn* kept pickled snakes and other curios on the counter. *Woolpack* and *Drover's Rest*, *Cumberland Wrestlers* and *Two Highland Laddies* ensured the people of Carlisle had reminders of their colourful past.

The impending end of the state monopoly in brewing and supply of strong drink in Carlisle was announced in January 1971, the Home Secretary, in reply to a parliamentary question, saying it was the intention of the government to bring in legislation to wind up the scheme and dispose of its assets. Carlisle had been one of the areas singled out by the Minister of Munitions in the First World War as places where war workers were spending too much time and money on 'demon drink'. Lloyd George is reported to have said, 'We are fighting Germany, Austria and drink – and the greatest of these deadly enemies is drink.' The Carlisle and District State Management Scheme brewed local beer and supplied 149 public houses, 11 hotels, seven retail shops and two restaurants – plus a number of free trade customers such as clubs and hotels. About one thousand people were employed. The assets here and at a similar state-managed area in Cromarty totalled about £4.7 million.

The Eden District, including Alston, recorded almost two million visitors in 2005. It has been assessed by the District Council that they spent £147 million and supported the equivalent of 3,772 full-time jobs. Tourism, now the major industry in the Eden Valley, has evolved from the days when remote parts of the country were accessible only to those with the inclination and means to travel. In the mid-19th century the railway stimulated exploration by charging passengers a penny a mile. Coastal resorts sprang up, and then came the guide books – dozens, then hundreds of them – catering for a tourist trade that expanded rapidly after the 1870s, by which time the Eden Valley was served by rail. Visitor numbers in the area recovered well after a downturn created in 2001 by an outbreak of foot and mouth disease.

Long distance footpaths have been established which bring trade to those who provide bed and breakfast to visitors. The Pennine Way extends from Edale in Derbyshire to Kirk Yetholm in Scotland, a distance of 250 miles. The grandest section is in what used to be the eastern part of Westmorland: Birkdale (with its solitary farm), High Cup Nick and the village of Dufton in the Eden Valley. From here, the Pennine Wayfarer heading north has an unremittingly hard slog to the plateau of Cross Fell,

146   *A fell walker at Hilton, on the East Fellside.*

147   *Cow Green dam, upper Teesdale, in course of construction.*

148 *Alfred Wainwright, creator of the popular Coast to Coast Walk, the half-way point of which is Kirkby Stephen.*

followed by a steady descent to Garrigill and Alston.

Alfred Wainwright devised the Coast to Coast Walk in 1973, referring to Kirkby Stephen as an obvious staging post, 'a place for licking wounds and replenishing supplies'. The Eden Valley Way begins on the north bank of the river at Rockcliffe Marsh and extends to the river's source on Black Fell Moss, a matter of 91 miles if the walker has enough energy to take in the summit plateau of Wild Boar Fell. The Lady Anne Trail follows the progress of this 'queen' of the Dales from Skipton to her favourite castle at Brougham, near Penrith.

Among the most imaginative schemes has been the development by the North Pennines Heritage Trust of what remained of the Nenthead mine into a stimulating educational experience. Visitors are encouraged to operate a variety of waterwheels and, further up the little valley, are conducted along tunnels and tramways in a horse level built by the London Lead Company about 1815. Among the specialist walks is 'Exploring the Eden Viaducts', Smardale Gill, Merrygill and Podgill now being in the care of the Northern Viaduct Trust. Among the many minor – but pleasurable – attractions are the *Brief Encounter* cafe at Langwathby station, a pottery at Wetheriggs and a woollen mill at Armathwaite.

Those who ascend Mickle Fell from Hilton must heed a notice in bold red lettering relating to the Army's general training area which sprawls over 40,000 acres, taking in Musgrave Fell, Warcop or Middle Fell, Long Fell and Roman Fell. The range was developed during the Second World War at a cost of several million pounds, money being spent on miles of concrete roads, on tank parks and gun emplacements. In the area, and now ruined, was the hamlet of Burton, birthplace in 1508 of Christopher Bainbridge. He became Archbishop of York, was subsequently raised to the dignity of a Cardinal by Pope Julius II. Bainbridge died in Rome. Wherever you go in the Eden Valley and on the Northern Pennines you will be attended by the ghosts of the past.

Bibliography

Blake, Joyce and Brian, *The Story of Carlisle* (1958)

Burgess, John, and others, *Christians in Cumbria* (1982)

Clare, T., *Archaeological Sites of the Lake District* (1981)

Cumbria magazine (various issues)

Emett, Charlie, *William Mounsey and the 'Jew' Stone* (1990); *The Eden Way* (1990); *Eden Tapestry* (1995)

Emett, Charlie and Templeton, J.P., *Carlisle – People and Places* (2003)

Eyres, Patrick, *Lady Anne's Way* (1985)

Ffinch, Michael, *Penrith and the East Fellside* (1985)

Frankland, J.C., *Pendragon Castle* (leaflet, 2002)

Fraser, George MacDonald, *The Steel Bonnets* (1956)

Hamilton, John, *Mallerstang Dale* (1993)

Hayes, Gareth, *Odd Corners in Appleby* (2002)

Holmes, Martin, *Appleby Castle* (1974)

Jollies Cumberland Guide & Directory (1811)

Kirkby Stephen Library, *The Droving Tradition of the Upper Eden Valley* (n.d.)

Lindop, Grevel, *A Literary Guide to the Lake District* (1994)

Mannix & Whellan, *History, Gazetteer and Directory of Cumberland* (1847)

Marshall, J.D., *Portrait of Cumbria* (1981)

McIntire, W.T., *St Cuthbert's Church, Edenhall* (revised 1990)

Millward, Roy, and Robinson, Adrian, *The Lake District* (1970); *Cumbria* (1972)

Mitchell, W.R., *Pennine Lead Miner* (1979); *How They Built the Settle-Carlisle Railway* (1989)

Monkhouse, James Chris, *Langwathby Past and Present* (1991); *Wind of Change Blows Through Langwathby* (1996)

Myers, Alan, and Forsythe, Robert, *W.H. Auden, Pennine Poet* (1999)

Nicholls, Revd W., *The History and Traditions of Mallerstang Forest and Pendragon Castle* (1883)

Palmer, William T., *The Verge of Lakeland* (1938)

Parker, John, *Cumbria* (1977)

Ramsden, Douglas M., *Teesdale* (1947)

Riley, James F., *The Hammer and the Anvil* (1954)

Rollinson, William, *A History of Cumberland and Westmorland* (1978)

Shotter, David, *Roman North-West England* (1984)

Southworth, James, *Walking the Roman Roads of Cumbria* (1985)

Sowerby, R.R., *Historical Kirkby Stephen and North Westmorland* (1950)

Wainwright, A., *A Coast to Coast Walk* (1973)

Watt, James W., *Short History of Rockcliffe* (1952)

Wood, G. Gordon, *The Upper Eden Valley* (1968)

Index

Numbers in **bold** refer to illustrations